# POST ROAD

*SUBMISSION AND SUBSCRIPTION INFORMATION*

Post Road publishes twice yearly and accepts submissions in all genres.

• POETRY: Editor, Post Road, P.O. Box 15161, Cincinnati, OH 45215

• FICTION: Editor, Post Road, P.O. Box 590663, Newton Center, MA 02459

• NONFICTION: Editor, Post Road, 203 Bedford Ave., Brooklyn, NY 11211

• ALL OTHER SUBMISSIONS should be addressed to the section editor and sent to:
853 Broadway, Suite 1516, Box 85, New York, NY 10003

*

Subscriptions: Individuals, $16/year; Institutions, $32/year;
outside the U.S. please add $6/year for postage.

Distributed by B. DeBoer, Nutley, N.J.

PRINTED IN CANADA

website: www.webdelsol.com/Post_Road

# POST ROAD

**Founding Editors**
Jaime Clarke
David Ryan

**Art Editor**
Susan Breen

**Criticism Editor**
Hillary Chute

**Etcetera Editors**
Jaime Clarke
Alden Jones

**Fiction Editors**
Rebecca Boyd
Michael Rosovsky
David Ryan

**Nonfiction Editors**
Pete Hausler
Kristina Lucenko

**Poetry Editors**
Mark Conway
Anne McCarty

*Associate Poetry Editor:* Jeffrey Shotts

**Recommendations Editor**
Tim Huggins

**Theatre Editor**
David Ryan

**Copy Editor**
Heather E. Fisher

**Special thanks to:**
Marcelle Good
Colin Dennis

# Table of Contents

## Recommendations

## Etcetera

## Art

# Contributor Notes

**Julia Alvarez** is a poet, essayist, and fiction writer. She spent her early childhood in the Dominican Republic, emigrating to this country and language at the age of ten. In 1991, she published *How the García Girls Lost Their Accents,* which was selected a Notable Book by the New York Times and an American Library [Association] Notable Book, 1992. Her second novel, *In the Time of the Butterflies* was a finalist for the National Book Critics' Award in fiction in 1995. She is also the author of two other novels, *¡YO!* (1997) and *In the Name of Salomé* (2000); a collection of essays, *Something to Declare* (1999); four books of poetry: *The Housekeeping Book, The Other Side/El Otro Lado, Homecoming: New and Collected,* and *Seven Trees;* and two books for young readers: *The Secret Footprints* (2000) and *How Tia Lola Came to Visit Stay* (2001). She is a writer in residence at Middlebury College.

**Chloe Bland** is an M.F.A. student in fiction at Bennington College. She lives in Stony Creek, Connecticut.

**Julianna Baggott** is the author of the national bestseller *Girl Talk* (2001), as well as *The Miss America Family* (April 2002), and a book of poems, *This Country of Mothers* (2001). Her work has appeared in dozens of publications, including *Poetry, Best American Poetry 2000,* and *Ms. Magazine.*

**Jenny Browne** works as a poet-in-the-schools and freelance journalist in San Antonio, Texas. She has recent poems published and forthcoming in the *Marlboro Review, Kalliope, The Seneca Review,* and *Many Mountains Moving.* Her first collection, *Glass,* was published by Pecan Grove Press in 2001.

**Steven Church** was born and raised in Lawrence, Kansas. His hometown was not destroyed by a nuclear attack in 1983, but the TV movie "The Day After" was filmed there. He graduated from the University of Kansas with a B.A. in philosophy and has just recently finished an M.F.A . in fiction at Colorado State University. He lives in Fort Collins, Colorado, with wife, Rachel, and their son, Malcolm. His work has been published in *River Teeth* and is forthcoming from *Puerto Del Sol, Quarterly West,* and *Quarter After Eight.*

**Kenneth Cook** teaches creative writing and literature and is chair of the Arts & Letters Program at Prescott College in Arizona. His fiction, nonfiction, and poetry have been published in numerous journals, including *Witness, Shenandoah, Threepenny Review, American Short Fiction, Alligator Juniper,* and *Harvard Review.* His awards include an Arizona Commission on the Arts fellowship, two Pushcart Prize nominations, and residency fellowships to The MacDowell Colony, Yaddo, and Blue Mountain Center. He is currently finishing a cycle of stories and a novel, in which the characters in "Easter Weekend" figure prominently.

**Brian Komei Dempster**'s poems have appeared in *The Asian Pacific American Journal, Crab Orchard Review, Green Mountains Review, Gulf Coast, Ploughshares,* and *Quarterly West.* He is the editor of *From Our Side of the Fence: Growing Up in America's Concentration Camps* (Kearny Street Workshop, 2001).

**Paul Eberly** recently finished an M.F.A. in fiction at the Bennington Writing Seminars. He lives in Chicago and Albuquerque and in the air between the two. His stories have appeared in *Standards* and *Conceptions Southwest*.

**Chris Elam** is Editor-in-chief of *ArtKrush, the art magazine online*.

**Janet Fitch** is the author of *White Oleander*. Her short fiction has appeared in such journals as *Black Warrior Review, Room of One's Own,* and *Venice West Review*. A resident of Los Angeles, she was the 2001 Moseley Fellow at Pomona College, and taught at Squaw Valley Community of Writers in August 2002.

**Katie Ford's** poems have appeared in *Ploughshares, Colorado Review,* and *Partisan Review,* among other literary journals. She currently studies poetry and teaches creative writing at The University of Iowa. Her first book, *Deposition,* will be published by Graywolf Press in fall 2002.

**Sarah Fox** lives in Minneapolis, where she is a Bush Artist's Fellow, a teacher of poetry and creative writing, and the editor of *Fuori Editions*. She is a regular contributor to *Rain Taxi Review of Books,* and her poems have appeared in many magazines such as *Verse, Conduit, Spout, Luna, Spinning Jenny,* and others. Her first book, *Assembly of the Shades,* is forthcoming in fall 2002 from Salmon Publishing in County Clare, Ireland.

**Barry Gifford's** novels have been translated into twenty-two languages. His book *Night People* was awarded the Premio Brancati in Italy, and he has been the recipient of awards from PEN, the National Endowment for the Arts, the American Library Association, and the Writers Guild. David Lynch's film, *Wild at Heart,* based on Gifford's novel, won the Palme d'Or at the Cannes Film Festival in 1990, and Barry Gifford's novel *Perdita Durango* was made into a feature film in 1997. Gifford co-wrote with director David Lynch the film *Lost Highway,* also released in 1997. His most recent books include *The Phantom Father: A Memoir* (named a *New York Times* Notable Book of the Year); *Wyoming,* a novel (named a Best Novel of the Year by the *Los Angeles Times*), which has been adapted for the stage and film; and *American Falls: The Collected Short Stories* (New York: Seven Stories Press, 2002). Barry Gifford can be found at www.barrygifford.com

**Elizabeth Graver** is the author of a story collection, *Have You Seen Me?,* and two novels, *Unravelling* and *The Honey Thief.* Her stories have been included in *Best American Short Stories, Prize Stories: The O. Henry Awards,* and *The Pushcart Prize Anthology.* She teaches at Boston College.

**John Griesemer** is the author of the novel *No One Thinks of Greenland.* Also an actor, he's worked on Broadway, Off-Broadway, in TV and feature films. His fiction has appeared in magazines including *Boulevard, Gettysburg Review,* and *Threepenny Review.*

**John Wesley Harding,** Gentleman Musician, is just about to release his ninth album and finish his first novel. His real name is Wesley Stace.

**Claire Hero** is a graduate of the Writing Program at Washington University. Her work has appeared in *Boston Review, Willow Springs,* and *Pool.*

**Edward Hoagland** is the author of *African Calliope, The Courage of Turtles, Red*

*Wolves and Black Bears, Tugman's Passage,* and *Walking the Dead Diamond River.* He lives in Vermont.

**Takahiro Kimura** was born in 1965 in Tokyo, Japan, where he currently lives and works as an artist and illustrator. His work has been published and exhibited widely in Japanese and international venues. He began creating artwork inspired by the human face in 1992, a subject that has most recently been explored in the *Broken 1000 Faces* series, begun in 1999.

**Justin Lane** is a photographer in New York City. His pictures from September 11 were among those awarded the 2002 Pulitzer Prize for Breaking News Photography.

**Norman Lock** has written for the American and German stage, German radio, and for film. A recipient of the Aga Kahn Prize from *The Paris Review,* he also writes short fiction.

**Robert Lopez** lives in New York, where he teaches at the New School. His fiction has appeared in *BOMB, New Orleans Review, The Chattahoochee Review,* and *American Letters & Commentary* and is forthcoming in *Neotrope* and *Confrontation.*

**Michael Moon** teaches American literature and queer theory at Johns Hopkins. He is the author of *A Small Boy and Others: Imitation and Initiation in American Culture from Henry James to Andy Warhol* (Duke, 1998) and *Disseminating Whitman* (Harvard, 1991).

**Stewart O'Nan**'s faster novels are *Snow Angels, The Speed Queen,* and *A Prayer for the Dying.* The slow ones, which he likes better, are *The Names of the Dead, A World Away* and *Everyday People.* His latest, *Wish You Were Here,* is really slow. He promises the next one will be quicker.

**Tim Parrish** is the author of *Red Stick Men,* a collection of stories set in and near Baton Rouge, Louisiana. He was nominated by Tim O'Brien for *Best New American Voices 2002.* He teaches at Southern Connecticut State University.

**Tom Perrotta** is a screenwriter and the author of the collection *Bad Haircut* and the novels *Election* (made into the acclaimed 1999 movie), *The Wishbones* and, most recently, the national bestseller, *Joe College.*

**Nelly Reifler**'s stories have been published by (or are forthcoming in) magazines, including the *Florida Review, BOMB, Mississippi Mud, Exquisite Corpse* and *Art on Paper;* you can also see Nelly's work at failbetter.com and exquisitecorpse.org; *Pressed Wafer* printed an excerpt of her novel-in-progress as a broadside; and she is one of the writers included in the anthology of post-9/11 literature *110 Stories* (NYU Press). Last winter, Nelly curated "What Happened in Lime Mills?," an exhibition based loosely on some of her writing, at the Rotunda Gallery. For several years, she co-edited the microzine *Aceldama* with her husband, artist Josh Dorman. Nelly has won U.A.S. Explorations and Henfield Prizes. Her collection, *See Through,* will be published by Simon and Schuster in 2003.

**Lauren Sandler** lives in Brooklyn. A former NPR producer and fellow of NYU's Cultural Reporting and Criticism program, she writes about American media and culture for *The Nation, Salon, The Los Angeles Times, The Village Voice, Newsday,* and *The New Republic,* among other publications.

**Elizabeth Scanlon** is associate editor of *The American Poetry Review* and a 2002 Pennsylvania Council on the Arts fellow. She lives in Philadelphia.

**Ashley Shelby** recently received an M.F.A. in nonfiction writing from Columbia University. She is most recently published in *Gastronomica: the journal of food and culture, Small Spiral Notebook, Mr. Beller's Neighborhood,* and *Carve Magazine* and has work forthcoming in *Watchword Literary Magazine* and *Transit* (U.K.). She lives in New York.

**Mary Sullivan** is the Coordinator for PEN New England. She spent the last year in Ouagadougou, Burkina Faso, where she and her husband read the Bible out loud. She is the author of the novel, *Stay.* ✧

# CRITICISM

POST ROAD

# Hip Hop High: Mainstream Black Culture in the White Suburbs

Lauren Sandler

In the Dean's office of Sachem High School in Ronkonkoma, Long Island, three clean cut boys lean back on folding chairs that line one wall of the lemon-painted room. One boy fidgets with strings of fine gold chain that hang around his neck, another bends over to tie the laces of his Fila high tops, another bounces one leg frenetically inside his huge Tommy Hilfiger jeans. He slumps back, staring at a sign that hangs over the secretary's desk. Written in blue script on 8x10 white paper, the sign reads: "NOT Yo, I need... INSTEAD Hello, Mrs. Batterberry, may I please have... thank you."

Outside the Dean's office, the locker-lined hall teems with white boys swaggering to class in baggy name-brand clothing and baseball hats pushed far back on their heads. Girls toss their blow-dried hair, spewing giggles and reproachful gossip from glossy lips, their gold chains sparkling at the necklines of tight brightly colored tops. Thirteen students—one of Sachem's peer mediation groups—trickle into a classroom to discuss teen issues. Today the students are talking about hip hop.

"Everyone I know listens to hip hop," says Gina, a Sachem senior in a tight purple sweater and iridescent eye shadow, sighing matter-of-factly. Her classmates murmur and nod in agreement. Gina continues, "It's not a statement. It's not what our lives are about. So I like Method Man, Biggie, DMX, whatever. Who doesn't? This isn't political; it's just what we all know."

For several years now, a mass of suburban white teens has dedicated their allowances to the consumption of hip hop. This group far and away leads sales of gangsta rap, almost completely replacing rock as the sound-track of choice at rec-room parties, in borrowed cars, and in second-floor bedrooms across America. Nightly news magazines hold segments on these kids they call "wiggas" (i.e. white + "nigga"); parents run confer-ences in high school cafeterias and auditoriums to discuss how hip hop colors their children's behavior. White appropriation of black culture is hardly a new phenomenon; the white jazz-cats of the fifties terrorized mainstream culture with their hep vernacular and behaviors, as did white aficionados of funk and blaxploitation films throughout the disco era. But for today's suburban consumers, black culture pervades pop media with signifiers from a truly distant ghetto.

"It's probably what I get asked about most frequently, this baffled 'What's going on with white kids and hip hop' question," says Tricia Rose, director of African-American studies at NYU and the author of 1994's *Black Noise: Rap Music and Black Culture in Contemporary America*. "It's only a logical extension of a kind of relationship that already existed. There's a long history to this; it's not a new thing. What they did was bor-row the slang and dances in blackface and at some point they eventually severed their recognition that those were black gestures, I mean, that's Elvis for example. Much of fifties' rebellion is about white kids immers-ing themselves in black culture and making those codes not just black. Which is precisely what is happening now with hip hop."

But, of course, adopting the codes of hip hop isn't the same as intel-lectually engaging with the factors that sustain a culture while imprison-ing it in a system of inequity. There's Hip Hop the Revolution, and then there's Hip Hop the Corporate Commodity (and a nebulous and fre-quently debated area that bleeds between the two). As Bakari Kitwana, the author of the new book *The Hip Hop Generation*, wondered aloud about white suburban hip hop kids over the phone recently, "How down are they, really? Isn't this more like a fascination with Britney Spears?" With a devious chuckle, he answered his own question. "I think we know the answer in many of these cases." The hip hop mainstream of Sachem High hardly challenges his assumption. But unlike mere attention to the style cues of teen pop, here hip hop's goods pervade all aspects of quan-tifiable youth culture, from what Sachem's teenagers say to what they drink to what they drive to who they worship—but yet who they never quite want to become.

*

"Yo, yo! Shut up! My nigga's hittin' me up, yo!"
It is a chilly spring Friday night. Eighteen guys huddle in tight circles, smoking joints and cigarettes. Some lean up against their parents' cars, kicking back swigs of Hennessey. Every one of them is white. A black Honda Prelude rattles to the thumping bass of a Notorious B.I.G. track. A kid in an oversized red down vest perches on the edge of an open trunk, sipping from a bottle of Malibu he fished out from a clutter of Nike shoeboxes.

"Who's that?" he asks his friend, who peers out from a huge hooded sweatshirt and matching baseball cap, both emblazoned with Nautica's ubiquitous brand name.

The friend holds a cell phone to his ear and fiddles with a gold chain around his neck. "Yo, it's Manny," he says to the crew. "He wants to know where the party's at."

"Where the party's at" means "what parking lot are you claiming as territory tonight." And tonight, like many nights, the party's in the main parking lot at The Colony, an upscale gated development in Holbrook.

Holbrook, which this group jokingly refers to as "Holbrooklyn," is a middle class community in central Long Island. Holbrook is familiar American terrain, a landscape of two-lane highways and small neighborhood streets that twist their way into cul-de-sacs—the manicured dead-ends of suburbia. Strip malls dot the landscape at semi-regular intervals, interchangeably offering insurance offices, florists, and fast food joints.

The Colony lies off the expressway on a barren, newly developed highway, tucked away from Holbrook's suburban grid; to enter, you must be admitted by a guard in a white shingled guardhouse. The entrance is paved in cobblestones. To the right of the guardhouse is a landscaped pond. The development, a maze of white shingled siding and stucco, houses professionals and their children. The only non-white person on the grounds of the Colony tonight is the security guard.

Tonight, at The Colony, like in suburban parking lots all over America, the biggest problem is where to get beer. The supply of Malibu is drained, and the crew has already been turned down at the three nearest liquor stores. But while chugging a 40 would be nice, there's always a plentiful stash of weed to smoke instead. The group struts across the asphalt ribbon that winds through The Colony over to the basketball court, which lies about ten yards from the first clump of white townhouses. Under the lamplight, the guys gather to pass a couple of joints around. Their sneakers form a snug circle. Smoke curls and hangs over their short-cropped hair, sweatshirt hoods, and baseballs hats, lingering in the light like in a shot from a rap video. For a moment the mood is silent, somber, ritualistic. Then Tom cracks up, giggles leaking out of his nose with plumes of smoke, deepening into a belly laugh. The circle joins in; chortles crescendo to whoops and high fives.

"Yo! This is the dope shit, yo!"

"Nigga gettin' me *all* fucked up!"

"Yo, who wants to play some ball?"

An impromptu three-on-three breaks out, more a shoving match with occasional shots on net than a basketball game. The guys yell insults at each other's mothers and girlfriends, laughing hysterically. When a bottle shatters through the sound, everyone looks up more to see who was hoarding the stash than who made the mess. And then, the sound of the inevitable. The whiny creak of a screen door.

A bearded, heavy-set man in his early forties lumbers out to his back steps from the closest home to the basketball court.

"Shit. Not this motherfucker again," the guys quietly rumble, shifting from foot to foot.

"Hey," Mr. Grown-Up calls out. "I'm just here to warn you that I've called the cops. And if you don't want to get in some serious trouble, I urge you guys to get out of here. The cops will be here momentarily. I mean it."

Chris, a tall kid in a baggy red Eddie Bauer sweatshirt, lopes out from one of the circles. Chris is the star kicker—all-county, all-league—of Sachem's football team. He's an icon at the Sports Authority, where he works, at his high school where he is admired, and in this parking lot— his parking lot—a stone's throw away from the condo where his parents are currently sleeping. His stride is confident as he approaches the enemy. "Yo! Hey! I live here! I have as much right to hang with my friends as you do. Who the hell are you to call the cops on us? We're just hanging out."

"Yeah? Smoking pot and yelling and blaring rap all night? Just hanging out?" Mr. Grown-Up turns to go back inside his house. He hesitates, then tosses one last puzzled, angry comment over his shoulder. "Where the hell do you think you are? *Where* do you think you are?"


A black Acura Integra rolls into the parking lot, to whoops and hollers. A baby-faced kid in a Gap baseball hat and a yellow puffy vest gets out grinning. "Let's get this party started right," Manny declares.

"'Sup, brother?" says Chris, pulling Manny into a headlock. "We're waiting for the cops to show up. Bust this shit up. But we ain't leaving, a-ight?" Manny nods, and with a wide smile, turns up the track already blaring and thumping from his speakers.

Manny's uncle gave him a copy of Public Enemy's *It Takes a Nation of Millions to Hold Us Back* when he was five. "I was hooked," he says. "I was this little hip hop kid. Everyone thought it was ridiculous." While rap connects Manny and his buddy Dave, who have both been devoted to hip hop since they were children, it's at the same time the source of a mellow rivalry. It's the old showdown, Larry versus Magic, John versus Paul. For these guys it's two slain rappers: Biggie versus Tupac. And while Dave's reverence for the Notorious B.I.G is quiet ("just let Biggie play, man, it speaks for itself"), the crew crowds around the open windows of the car to taunt Manny as he preaches the gospel of Tupac.

"I really do think, I swear to God, I really do think he's alive." Manny's face is set in earnestness, his mouth tight, his gestures poised in contrast to the guys leaning casually into the car.

"Manny's wack, yo! Resurrecting Tupac. You're wack, boy!"

"Yeah, well he's got all these verses about resurrection, right? Like how he's coming back like Jesus?" Manny shakes his head, pushing his buddies out of the car. "You have to believe it. He's like the most emotional rapper. He's the realest." He starts thumbing through Dave's CDs, pausing quizzically when he finds one by Fleetwood Mac in a collection chock full of gangsta rap.

"That's for the *other* people, yo," Dave says, suppressing a shy giggle.

Manny laughs, but isn't distracted from his passion. He emotionally gestures at the pages of hip hop albums. "There's so many rappers who like talk about being like being the bad gangsta right? He's what's real. Everyone else pisses me off, like they know about thug life. But he's like the only one who grew up, he was poor, he was so poor it wasn't even funny and then like how he got into art and stuff like that, that's the Mac, man."

"Biggie's for real, too," Dave scowls, as Brian, the kid in the puffy red vest, climbs into the back seat.

"Yeah, but check out this track." Manny rolls up the windows, and turns up the volume. The three boys sit silently, nodding gravely to the beat in perfect unison. This isn't good-time music. This isn't a rock and roll party. It's funereal, foreboding, a sermon in a dark and thunderous church.

Automatic gunfire makin' all my enemies run.
Who should I call when I'm shot and bleedin'.
Indeed the possibility has part a chase in cream.
Dope got me hatin' fiends. Scheme wit my team, just a chosen few.
My foes victim of explosives. Come closer. Exhale the fumes.
We got memories fadin' fast. A slave for cash.
Accelerate, mash, blast, then dash.
Don't look now. How you like it, raw.
Niggas ain't ready for the wrath of the outlaws. Never surrender.

"Awesome," Manny whispers at the end of the track. "I mean, I don't relate to it at all. I know it doesn't have anything to do with me. I mean, like a while ago, like two years ago when he died, I was really caught up in it. I was like way into it. I wasn't acting like a thug—well not too much, but it was a phase of me really wanting to be black and dressing like it and shit like that. But I couldn't be farther from this. I mean, look where we are. Right?"

He flips off his baseball cap and ruffles his short-cropped brown hair. "But it's not like I would trade my life in for Tupac's life. Hell no. Not for a minute. No way. I have it made. I get everything I want except for a car. That's the only thing that's holding me back right now. I'm getting paid for college, and I didn't even do good in school." Manny doesn't feel like he has a lot to rebel against. Unlike Dave and most of these guys, he's close to his parents, even occasionally opting to spend evenings with the family instead of with his friends.

Although Manny's parents are both professionals and his suburban lifestyle is secure and comfortable, they are a world away from the envy-spawning material excess of your average hip hop video—excess that generates swells of admiration in the hearts of these young consumers. "The only reason we like them so much is look how they prosper, right?" Manny says, looking to Dave for assent. "They have everything. Check their videos. It's crazy. The cars, boats, bitches. I mean, the *hottest* cars, yo. It's so like you just *want* it. You figure listening to it, getting into it—not like you wanna be like them—just like you envy them. It's awesome."

Dave nods. "Exactly."

Manny continues. "But I'd never even go to the hood. Anywhere like that. Fuck that. Especially being white. "

Dave keeps nodding. "No way. I'm with you. Why would I go there?"

Shyly, Brian says, "I'd go. I would. I wouldn't walk around, but I'd drive through. Wouldn't you check it out?"

Dave furrows his brow and pauses to see if Brian is serious. "Hell, man. No way." He sweeps his hand over his CDs. "I've got it all here."


What other art form than music—whether high-brow, low-brow or no-brow—spins such a web of cultural codes? The intensive co-mingling of music and lifestyle, paired with white America's fascination with black America, has led a previous generation down this path of slang and sub-version. In the fifties, legions of clean-scrubbed white kids shocked their parents with their mania for jazz, and all the late night, reefer-smoking carnality and danger that such music represented. But in the decades since, the dissemination and consumption of urban culture has entirely changed. For Manny, Dave, and their generation of suburban consumers of urban experience, black culture comes shrink-wrapped and consumer-ready at chain stores like Coconuts and on MTV. One needs to venture no further than the local mall or the family den to access neatly packaged urbanism. In the fifties, when white youth famously explored the jazz dens and blues bars of America, the experience was a radically different one. Exploration mandated a literal departure from familiar suburban enclaves.

Norman Mailer was hip to the differences between detached consumption and active participation. In his 1957 essay "The White Negro: Superficial Reflections on the Hipster," he wrote: "In such places as Greenwich Village, a ménage-à-trois was completed—the bohemian and the juvenile delinquent came face-to -face with the Negro." Mailer clarifies, "So there was a new breed of adventurers, urban adventurers who drifted out late at night looking for action with a black man's code to fit their facts. The hipster had to be absorbed in the existential synapses of the Negro." For today's suburban hip hop kids there is largely no such physical co-mingling of black and white—no literal adventuring. Instead the immersion takes place in a media existence of black culture that functions as a sort of virtual tourism.

Likewise, the techno-explosion of mass media, and consequently the successful mass-marketing of hip hop, has placed this commercialized arm of urban black youth culture squarely in the mainstream. "The music is really at the center of American youth culture now in a way it hasn't been," says Tricia Rose. "As opposed to being simply black American youth culture, [hip hop] actually has usurped rock as the ubiquitous symbol of white male youth." For Mailer's hipsters, an obsession with black culture was significant precisely because it was obsession with a subculture. This is exactly what he saw as fundamental to what he perceived as the radicalism of that generation of white youth. Mailer lamented an era imprisoned in conformity, "where security is boredom and therefore sickness"; he suggested that the escape from that prison was through immersion in a kind of outlaw black culture. It is easy to update his descriptions of the hipsters of the fifties to the hip hop kids of modern-day suburbia; superficially, the antecedents are uncanny. Yet, according to Mailer, these hipsters were radicals, engaging not just in recreational teenage rebellion, but in a full-out ideological assault on middle class values.

Of course, this sort of cultural immersion is hardly synonymous with political radicalism—and Mailer's black culture fetish has provoked cries of racism from readers (including this one) since the publication of his controversial essay. However, Mailer's ethic represented a start; at least back then there was face-to-face appeal, a desegregating of the physical space of the club, not just an expensively shot and edited lifestyle viewed as pixels in the comfort of a suburban development. And at this point in hip hop's narrative—twenty years since its birth as an underground culture, ten years into its commodification as mass culture, it is hard to see much power lying in what Mailer describes as subcultural subversion of conventionality. "Almost any kind of unconventional action often takes disproportionate courage," he wrote. Hip hop's commercial ubiquity vacates today's white teens of what Mailer deemed to be the source of revolutionary power. Because today's white suburban hip hop devotees seem largely to know nothing about the politics of how their heroes land in jail, for example, hip hop represents no social subversion in gated communities like those in which the Sachem crew parties.

Like Manny says, these teenagers grew up with rap; they were born in the days following the first turntable scratches of the late seventies. Growing up with rap takes away the thrill of discovery, of dangerous liberation, that accompanied freestyling, break-dancing, graffiti-spraying b-boys who are now well into their thirties. White writer and performance artist Danny Hoch describes the difference between discovering hip hop on subways and in underground clubs back in the day, a stark contrast to discovering it at the mall. "It used to be that you had to

*These teenagers grew up with rap; they were born in the days following the first turntable scratches of the late seventies.*

get up on the train, get into a fight, run from the police, just to get your groove on. It was an active resistance," he recalls. MC Serch of the white rap duo 3rd Bass talks about the death threats he received just for dressing in a hip hop style and speaking hip hop slang—before he even deigned to pick up a microphone. These experiences speak to the sort of cultural risk-taking Mailer describes as central to any cultural revolution; in many cases, they supercede his idiom. When one is actually immersed in someone else's social sphere, it's difficult to ignore the systemic political and economic issues that spawn that culture of resistance.

Not so with our current "white negroes." Driving Dad's car to the mall for the new DMX CD promoted on the cover of *Rolling Stone* at newsstands everywhere is hardly a previous decade's equivalent of jumping a barbed wire fence in the projects to be one of the only white kids at a word-of-mouth rap show. Being chased by cops from one parking lot to the next represents no significant civil disobedience for teenagers like Manny.

Saturday night we come as close as we'll get to Mailer's world of interracial immersion in these Long Island suburbs. The convoy of parent-owned cars speeds past Carvel, past Ronkonkoma Plumbing and Heating Supply, and down a maze of dark suburban roads that bear storybook names like Tulip Street, Magnolia Avenue, and Prince Charming Road. The cars pass near a recent addition to the Sachem district, a tree missing a significant chunk of its trunk, where a car plowed into it several months before, taking the lives of the kids in the car with it. The tree is adorned with bandanas, their color streaked and faded by wind and rain. The bandanas represent solidarity among Sachem's "gangs," who wear different colors to claim their "set," a declaration modeled on the behavior of inner-city gangs across America. In the past year, Sachem has lost thirteen members of its graduating class.

The group pull their cars up in front of a two-story house with a gigantic white Lincoln Navigator out front. Screams and yells compete with the hard thud of the bass pumping from the living room.

"Yo! Keep it down! We can't have the cops coming!" yells a tall, heavy-set black kid with an unkempt short afro, in a white and burgundy Colorado State football jersey. "They call my parents and I'm fucked, man! All of this," he yells, "means I don't get this"—he gestures to the gold-detailed Navigator in the driveway.

"What up, Ariel," the gang passes by their host, beating him with back-slaps and high-fives. "Yo, yo, my nappy-haired brother," one of the guys giggles. "Shit, brother, it's a PAAARTYYYY!"

Cherry red shag carpeting runs through every room on the first floor —including the kitchen—and up the stairs to the bedrooms. A wrought-iron gate separates the entryway from the cluttered living room, where a faux-Victorian couch and side chairs dominate, upholstered in sky-blue velvet and covered in plastic. The room is crammed with houseplants in macramé planters, a marble coffee table, an organ, a wheel chair, an exercise climber, shelves of family pictures, and stacks of unmarked cardboard boxes. Rhymes from an Onyx CD bounce off the walls—three stucco, one mirrored.

Three black guys gather around an old plastic boom box next to the foyer. With the exception of their nervous host, they are the only black kids at the party. They lean into each other—their shoulders forming a tight oval that blocks out the frenetic behavior of the white kids around them—and start freestyling over the Onyx track. Shaqwan leads the group. He is a perpetually sober and reassuring but threatening presence at these parties. As one kid says, "Shaqwan is peaceful, but he'll kill ya to keep the peace." He picks up the beat, staring fixedly at his hands that slice the air before him in punctuating gestures. His rhymes speak directly to what surrounds him:

Respect the race in your face
United front I never ever smoke a blunt
Never take a drink and never will I got my fill
And word up look around the room at these kids with their pills.

This circle seems oblivious to the other kids in the room; they're separated from their screams and giggles. "YEAH, I'M THE REAL PIMP," a beefy white guy in a baseball hat hollers over the heads of the circle of freestylers to a pasty-faced friend on the other side. The friend raises his beer and yells over their rhymes, "YOU KNOW IT, NIGGA."

I doubt this party is what Norman Mailer had in mind when nearly fifty years ago he imagined the effect of mainstreaming black urban youth culture. "With this possible emergence of the Negro, Hip may erupt as a psychically armed rebellion," he wrote, "and bring into the air such animosities, antipathies, and new conflicts of interest that mean the empty hypocrisies of mass conformity will no longer work." Now there's simply a new hypocrisy of mass conformity in baggy pants and identity-crashing slang.

Yet Danny Hoch sees possible redemption in this generation of white hip hop fans: he regards black mass culture as the closest shot at radicalism in today's suburbs. "Because there is no apparatus in education in suburban locales for activism, for rebellion, they have to create their own *sense* of revolution. The only tool they can find is a cultural tool, it's picking up the new Jay-Z album. And through accessing hip hop cultural tools they are at least opening a resistance to the status quo." Hoch also sees how hip hop has positively influenced the actions of his generation of X-ers. "I don't think we knew metaphors of resistance until we started to read the *Village Voice* or went to college. But now my peers and myself are lawyers and teachers and are trying to make collective change alongside black and Puerto Rican people who also have gone through this, who are now editing magazines and directing firms," he says. "My hope is these kids who don't understand the political relevance of banging DMX in Dad's Audi, thinking that they are keeping it real, my hope is that when these kids go to college they will organize, take the spirit of resistance and not be passive."

Hoch's vision for the future of white hip hop fans does not necessarily correspond with their own sense of the next stage of their lives. Jen— a girl whose face is often set in the grimace of an exasperated homeroom teacher—has the frustrated expectation that her time at SUNY Cortland will be a replication of her high school experiences. Maybe high school—and even college—simply does not provide the intellectual tools to deconstruct the constant strobe of the media world. To Rose, this is just the issue. "The hope is limited to me—especially by the access of any public education on black people," Rose says. "Do they actually have any sense of the history of race in the United States in relation to the largest issues in history? Any idea? And if the answer to that is 'no,' then I don't see how the music can underwrite that level of ideological domination....If they don't understand why there is a ghetto in the first place, why it keeps getting reproduced," she shakes her head and laughs bitterly, "if they don't have any knowledge about that, *what's Jay-Z gonna do about it?*"

Jen checks her beeper, adjusts her jacket, and applies lip gloss. Her pale blue eye shadow and dark eyeliner draw attention to her moon-shaped face. She cuts an athletic figure at just under six feet. Like many of the guys in the crowd, Jen is an athlete; tennis in the fall, basketball in the winter, and volleyball in the spring. Her gas and lipstick money comes from working at Lady Foot Locker in the Smithhaven Mall. Smoking her cigarette, she weaves through groups of guys to a patch of her friends shivering in Ariel's backyard. "Did you catch how Jim like totally ignored me at Taco Bell? I just tried to talk to him and he totally blew me off. I can't wait 'til he calls me and says come over and sleep with me baby. Manny, you oughta try to talk to him and get him on track. I tried to talk to him, but he wouldn't even look at me."

The guys look around, shuffle their feet. She tries again. "Anyone check out the new Black Rob CD?"

Matt perks up. "Yeah. It's the hype."

Stoney shuffles up to Jen and Matt, grinning. "Hey, anyone got a menthol cigarette?"

"Sorry, honey," Jen says.

"Where you going to school, anyway?" asks Stoney.

"Cortland," she replies. "Who isn't? Shit, we're leaving Sachem to go to Sachem. It won't be no different. Wherever we go we'll find parking lots and get drunk and rap and the cops will show up and we'll go home. Right?" Jen shakes her head and surveys the party. "Hell, what do I know. My dad never finished college and my mom never went. They're not exactly letting me know what to expect. I'm on my own."

"Yo, whatever." Stoney ambles over to the next clump of kids, his baggy khakis dragging on the ground. "Yo, what up, brother? You got a menthol cigarette?" ✧

# POETRY

POST ROAD

# Twin Cities, No Sign

Jenny Browne

Before every well-insulated house
a car breathes with no body.

I follow the three-pronged
pace of the winged, head

for the circling gray, one
of a thousand lakes, days, walks.

My boots are heavier than usual,
heavier than boots.

Even the slush hushing
*too much, too much*

of this human filling up
and in, opposite of tree

branches skinny and scratched
black against sky.  Blurry line

between lake and lifetime.
But don't send the search party

out for my voice.  I know it
takes two full inches of ice

to hold a body. I'm just edgy,
following the hidden bank, following

the ink-dipped goose ends,
surfacing buoys of belief

in the beneath.  Half a being
broken by another

snowflake's circle changing
the surface without a sound.

# Before

**Jenny Browne**

the yellow pine floor was *done,*

then mopped, carpets flopped,
warped windows

shaking as the spin cycle begins

there was another place
and footprints
before boards Wind
before breathing Leaves
glittering in the back-light

Out front a telephone pole leans
into lost voices

They painted this porch ceiling
to look like sky
but now the pale
blue is peeling free

The bees were never fooled

Someone missed the corners
Left cloud  Left cloud

# It's Late Here How Light Is Late Once You've Fallen

Katie Ford

I began to see a gauze over the wheat.
The fields were darker where an owl had flown
against the window of the house. I bent
and put my fingers into its cold down. Hundreds
of tiny spiders unhinged their bodies, bodies
which are their minds, as my body was,
moving like a city wanting to go inside
all the cavities. Moths too,
some were caught and tried to flutter out. I put my hands in
farther. Felt the body of the thing, the owl. At first it seemed
so dead. Then, not at all—either my fingers
pulsing with blood or its breathing. I held
breath too, like a mother bent to the crib. Nothing.
Then maybe something. I looked behind me,
my fingers making out bones, twigs of what was left, glazed
by faint morning stars that pocked the sky when I looked up, stars
in their arc of recovery from being seen
into being hidden again by light. Some of its feathers
were matted. When it had hit the window
the storm layers shook the space between. *Lie still*, I said to you,
*I'll go see.* But all I really wanted
was to leave that house, your
steady rise and fall of breathing inside it.
Outside, there was no farther in to go. It must have been
a barn owl with its heartish face
and lightly speckled underneath, its feathers
thin leaves spotted with mold. I pulled out my hands
and spread its wings out full, the soft body
exposed. And that's when I was sure it was dead—
when it let me do that to its body.

# Elegy to the Last Breath

Katie Ford

The heron in the marsh extends
its striped neck its dagger-bill points into the sky during its long sleep

it will be mistaken for a reed I had nothing
to hide by I had to move my body instead

into a space
that was not a space between the fallen-down wall and the grass

cement and grass pressed against my lungs collapsing
if owls fly among the ruins as it is written I had nothing to see them
with

grass had no room to shudder corridors flattened
in the dirt like veins pinched off by weight

Lord of harvest and of land if you commanded this
rest now it has come to pass.

# Shadow of the Valley

Sarah Fox


Blessed be the birds for they will be blown
away and burned.  Complete.  Multiplied
by the first language of wind,
abandoned nests cling to elastic branches.
Vibrating, vegetal.  An ice blue
trill cramps with a prodigal twilight.
What is the ration?  Charred mid-flight.
The bones of them.
Swept sparrows lit at the altars
in blessed leafy gutters.
Left at the steps with a lidful glare.
Pink in them.  Spices. Our hearts
swell with a feeling of finished
wings, at last we revere them
utterly.  Flying
into caves. They have air
to make sounds with, to soar on,
then they do not have it
any longer. Blessed
be the nimble sound of a crow.
Birds batting at the door and in hair,
blessed be the blight of them we
flee from. A thousand birds
skewed east like divers poised
at the rim.  Blessed be the hysterical
utterance of sound in the mouths
of creatures. Clocks yet stopped
at the very hour, finches flying  past
explode within that round conclusion.
A solitary dove then swoons
into circles of absentia so brief
as to be silver. As to feed
the bits of calendar back to its worm.

Each wind begins with the arrival
of birds.  Such a silver
fur on our skyline. Blessed
for we love them though they will not
stop to save us. Yes
an intimate future leafs through
our fingers, flies off. Think of how tired
their little wings. Caught in the eye
of a storm they ended up mistakenly.
The gauzy cut-outs, have you ever autopsied
a bird?  Had papery x-ray
daydreams?  An obstinate palsey
hangs over the people. How many
trees on this horizon?  How do they choose
where to land?  The smoke of it.
Endless fields of flutter, hawing.
Cooing.  The low-flying pigeons
clothed with the sun, their stupid labor.
Smudges of poverty become bells
tied to their skinny talons.
Is it sad that babies cannot
distinguish a bird from a plane?
Blessed be the babies, with eyes full of wing.
Fallen, fallen.  Write this down:
happy are the dead who die.
Their hum won't be returning.
The little beating, beyond terrains of sound,
little efforts.  And blazes resembling
documents.  The beloved's wings
empty over a heaviness, a night of
no one sleeping.  Pray for the lack
of it, blessed be anguish. The clouds
part so politely for this theatre.
Here is the quickening cluster,
or are we still watching tv?
Blessed be levitation
for it shall yield a downpour.

Scald-crow, raven, carrions,
laser-browed hawks, street
roosters, swallows, the blood
dart of cardinals, gaggles, bastions and rookeries,
ostriches striding the desert, the hummingbird—
how we esteem each blessed delicacy.
Was there anything like a ghost
in their tilting? So early in the fever,
the fable of fury and wings
unfolding before the advancing night.
Does it hurt to crash down from the sky?
Blessed be the phantom limb of destiny.
Do you know you are glad you were born?

# How To Get The Love You Want

Sarah Fox


Hold my whispers.
I have the impression that father
knows the way home.
The wheel hears its harness.
Hauls its dusk through aisles
of bent crows. The horse's
shadow canters sidelong
up the gate, into the neighbor's
plum grove. His tail twitches
at snowflakes as if they were
bitter flies. He is as if blindfolded.

Truth is plain. Like a prairie.
Like a little house
between heaven and earth.
A horse in the yard.
Crows on the roof.
Snow heaving against the doorway
like grown men hoisting a wall.
Inside the house father
tells stories, smokes a pipe.
Mother reads a letter close to the fire.

If I were busy I would have sparks.
Darkness would resist me,
blindfolds would run like India ink
down the faces of strangers.
They would become stained.
If I would read the letter
in my little house, tend the fire.
If I rode the horse into the woods,
chasing the wheel as it goes and goes.

It is unimaginable to be a horse,
isn't it? Or a wheel, to be never
upright for long. Winter is sweet.
It slows us in our tracks. We lope
from fire to fire. Our hope
whispers through its blindfold.

# Graffiti

**Brian Komei Dempster**

Inside a toilet stall, I find secrets
made glaring with ink, followed

by the numbers of those I imagine dialing:
Hal, the janitor whose eyes trail down us

like suds; Mr. Stanton, who suspends me
twice for smoking pot; and Mr. White,

the gym teacher who models for Sears
and autographs the catalogues for girls.

I try to guess who wrote *Go team go*
beneath star quarterback, Chip Fuller,

and his girlfriend, Julie, her cheerleader
breasts with enormous nipples.  I suspect

Chip came up with the slogan
*Joey Finley, four-eyed sissy who can't get*

*any KUNT.*  I hunt until I find the most
flamboyant boys *—Baryshnikov, suck my cock—*

Billy Crescent in his tights, practicing
pirouettes for the next Nutcracker,

and Joey each time he backs away
from a pass.  The buck-toothed, slit-eyed drawing

is meant to be my mother.  I fight
to see the caption *Go home Jap bitch*

through the blue eyes of Chip, to know
his touch for winning, praised by a handshake

from Mr. Stanton, a pat on the back
from Mr. White.  I need to feel

the aching which shrouds the room
where Hal pulls his mop over the floor

while Chip and his teammates knead
Ben Gay into stiff limbs, ease joints

with ice and tape, envious while
they listen to how Chip is going

to take Julie doggie style in his basement,
or the back of his father's car, hold her face

against anything that muffles the sound,
her silence like Joey's, like Billy's, like my mother's,

even mine, our silence in the words I smear
with the spit on my sleeve and begin to rub out.

# The Chain

Brian Komei Dempster

You swaggered with the girls you'd done and the girls
you wanted to do, *the virgins, the sluts, the prudes*
with red hair and freckles, your cock catching fire
in a forest of orange, or the blonde goddess

who didn't know our first names, flicking back
her hair while she blew smoke rings between classes,
and me bragging how this weekend it would be me
with Amber, her cross and the chain I'd unclasp,

when she popped, the cherry stain, and after
I stuffed the sheet in the hamper, how sore she would be
when I left her in bed, her underwear on the post,
she'd wake without a note, without a phone call,

and I added her to our chain of names which grew
during gym class between glimpses at the boys
you called *flamers*, Billy Crescent who'd never know
how to mount the way we did, except the missionary,

and only with a boy, not with boys like us, how I shivered
to picture him, giving it or taking it, so convenient
to forget him, to block out my feigned belief
in Amber's Jesus who told her to wait, and we did,

but instead I was proud to lie to you, it seemed
I did have sex each week, each score another level
on *the food chain* you called it, each cliché
a variation on the last, *She went down on me so long*

*she was gasping* the lines we learned rewinding
the VCR in your basement where you laid newspaper
across your parents' rug, *For practice* you said,
*to be the one who lasts* but I hoped I knew the real reason

our cocks were jackhammers in our Vaselined fists
side by side with a speaker between us, my hands
going up and down, an imagined mouth, first Amber's,
then Billy's, maybe the o of his lips slightly bigger,

maybe behind the cover of pines Billy's act
more secret, hurried, we were lost when
we came, unaware of your parents' key turning
in the front door, why didn't Billy hear the boys

in the park with chains around their fists,
the links which sent him to intensive care,
later in the auditorium the way you whispered *fairy*
into my ear and this time, I didn't turn my head

or nod instead taking in Billy as he leapt
and spun across the stage, merged into the girls,
each movement soothing me, his eye
bruised dark as steel beneath the eye patch,

the flesh lashed red beneath his tights,
his grace hiding the remnants of violence,
your scoff when I told you I would face Amber,
and when I did, it was much different,

something about commitment to God, being true
to her too, my white lie like a sin straight
to her face, beneath the blanket, how she was
the first and only one I would ever make love to,

even as the others began to blur into me, ready
to pretend she was them, or not them at all, only a glimmer
of you and the gang of boys as her cross dangled
above my mouth, linking her to me, shifting the chain.

# Marginalia

Claire Hero

The pages of the book we bought
are stippled with rain, seeded with pollen and ash.
In the closed eye, you sit
beneath a hazel tree, wreathed in green
and reading among the rooks.

Yesterday takes the form of rooks
hunched on my highest branches.
Little treacheries.

This morning I watched a woman dance with a red fan.
She was aged. Starlings nested in her hair.
"I know the dark and song of you," said the curve of her arm.
"I know your windowless room,"
said her knee. Her good eye snapped shut.
What gift storm carried me here?

You take my finger, drag it across the page,
and the words form wings, flutter beneath my skin,
flutter around the stones in my chest.
"This is forgiveness," you tell me.
It flaps in every open door.

# Divination

**Claire Hero**

If you wake to crows squawking
in the open space behind your last dream, it is best

to call it luck. To protect from misfortune,
stitch ash-petals to your underclothes. And if you find yourself

submerged in a glass box, toss your open face
to the back of the closet.

In the Office of Calamitology they have filed away, safely,
your first love, your last breath.

You may find them there, squeezed among the files
of First Word, Lost Button, Missing Tooth.

Everything is safe, somewhere.
If you stand on a pier tossing tulips into the islands of the Atlantic,

you are almost beautiful. Fish once thought extinct
will gather at your feet, and in their phosphorescence

you will see how far you've traveled by bone and lung.
There are no nets where you are going.

# Closing Time

Elizabeth Scanlon

> & my very close companion
> gets me fumbling gets me laughing
> she's 100 but she's wearing something tight
> —*Leonard Cohen*

The line wonders why it is there.
A point on the line, a point there—
why here, him there,
the clothes of proper demeanor
look good on you, you never
look so good as when showing your age
a good time.
And on shoulders rest
the mantle of life.
Minky stole, steal away, make it
out all right.
The smack, sigh, the undone slide
deranges nuns & starlets
peopling what's called
consciousness. Nessy-ness,
o punishment of the flesh. Their eyes float
two paces behind & six feet above
themselves in the procession.
I'd call it guilt if it didn't suit so well.

# Quarry

**Elizabeth Scanlon**

A day comprised:
       Waking—scent & leaving—blur,
       lights & trains—you miss, you crowd,
       wet woolen skin abrasions,
       the eros of influence, *thwocketa thwocketa*
       those wheels in the tracks, such
       quandary.
We'd swim in cold danger, trespass
       backwoods border state past-
       time, skinny dip the quarry hole
       gone spring-fed, wide & fathomless
       deep, its edges more eroded
       every dive, each re-visit.

In my day we had.
It's been raining for days.

The un-understood a food never craved;
misunderstanding just a numb tongue.
Still shelved, not sought, bought, put to use.
The wooden floor smell is there, dollars desires &
dry goods. Comes to mind but is not quite.
Not clothed. Not naked.
But much as wet goods
once had meaning—
binding paint, olive oil, liquor
in unity, so this.

Desire like water,
how is it owned?
(There is the *water company*, yes, they bill.)
The rain carried inside,
black umbrella drawn in

with a little *thwick* in the portico.
Trailing what's gathered passing through.
Amidst yet ignorant of the nature of you.

The odd occasion of intersection, a great reward.
Who even asked directly to tell you it's hideous, won't.

**THEATRE**   POST ROAD

# Beyond Recognition: A Monologue in 12 Sections

Norman Lock

For Nicholas Lock and Gordon Lish

CHARACTER

A MAN 30–50. He is blindfolded and bound to a chair.
He is dressed in pajamas.

I.

*(Silence, then:)*

MAN

Where to begin?

*(Pause)*
It began
yesterday, or the day before I

*(Irresolutely)*
It's difficult the passage of time is difficult
to tell

If I could feel my face
if I could feel how bad I need a shave
whether there's a beard I could tell how long
something anyway, a guess, an
estimate—that would be something, a beard
as it is it's hard to say how long I've been here
with your eyes covered, it's hard, and the fact that there's no sound,
    nothing but silence
is also difficult

But let's say it's been two days
two or three—three days at most I've been like this
three days ago I came down to—this is important

*(Irresolutely)*
I think it's important
three days ago I came down to breakfast and my wife said, "You're not
    yourself today."
I was sitting at the table spooning sugar into the cup
one, two spoonfuls of sugar, sitting there
at the table
not saying a word
I had a headache, my head was splitting
she sat across the table from me, watching what I was doing with the
    sugar

I looked up I
stopped stirring the coffee
I looked at her—"What do you mean?"

"Nothing it's just that—"
she shrugged, went back to buttering her toast
the way she buttered her toast always annoyed me
she used too much butter—that was one thing
and she spent an excessive amount of time spreading it around
because of all the butter, there was much too much of it
so she had to work it in, into the bread, the toast
with her knife
her butter knife
back and forth, back and forth
as if she were plastering a wall, I
it annoyed me

"What do you mean I'm not myself today?"

She shrugged again—first the right shoulder, then both shoulders
    together
I put down the spoon
it clattered against the saucer
loud, loudly
so that she'd know my mood, that I wasn't going to be shrugged off

"It's just an expression," she said,
"a figure of speech."

She was right
it was just an expression, one I'd heard before
many times
an innocent remark
I'm sure she didn't mean anything by it
it was just one of those phrases people use
you hear them all your life
but then
one day you hear it as if for the first time
really hear it
what it means and the world opens up dangerously
yawns in your face
and you're on the edge
the edge of the abyss
which is another expression—two, in fact
two figures of speech we've heard all our lives without really considering
    what they mean
and then suddenly you do
you do consider it
and, Christ, it's like the world opens up

which is what happened three days ago over breakfast

"What do you mean I'm not myself today?" I repeated

"Well, for one thing, you never come down to breakfast in your pajamas."

That's true, I don't

"You didn't shave this morning and you always do."

Also true
but that morning I couldn't stand the thought of it, didn't want to feel the
    sting of the water and
and that scraping
I had a headache, I was, in fact, hung over, I
I've been drinking lately
drinking, I mean, more than usual
down in the cellar
I'd taken to sitting down there nights, watching TV and drinking to get
    away from them a little while

I wanted
to think
and there was always such a racket, such a lot of noise
so for the last month or so I'd been going down the cellar after dinner to
    think and watch TV and get
not drunk
in a better frame of mind
that night I'd gotten into a wonderful frame of mind
my mind was
glistening

*(Silence)*
She was right, I wasn't my self, but then
if not myself
who
who was I?

Well, that's when it all began, I think
with that one simple observation of hers
a meaningless observation unmotivated by
she meant nothing, it was not malicious, simply it wasn't like me to come
    to breakfast unshaved and in my pajamas

I should have let it drop
I should have let the whole thing drop right there
but, like I said, the world opened up at that moment and I stared open
    mouthed at the abyss
looked it in the face
if I wasn't myself then who was I?

*(Silence)*

*(Laughs)*
It wasn't something I believed in, this idea that there's something
something inside
you can't see it, touch it, x-ray it, find it with a knife
you know what I'm talking about, don't you, this
I always believed in the body, the brain, the mind, memory—all that,
and that's what we are
that is what makes us who we are and different
but I haven't lost any of that

I haven't lost my mind or my memory
I still have my body, my brain still works
I'm talking, thinking
so what've I lost, what's missing exactly?

And yet I feel that something is
missing, something
essential
but I don't know what
not to be yourself—what does that mean *exactly*?

        *(Pause)*
What am I doing here?


I went outside to take some pictures
I like to take pictures, taking pictures is something that makes me happy
I went out after that disturbing conversation with my wife, left her to
    finish buttering her toast
I didn't bother to change
I went out in my pajamas
what did it matter? at that point it didn't matter one bit how I was dressed
I did have the presence of mind to put on my raincoat, my shoes—I'm not
    a complete idiot
it had been raining
it was a cold, damp morning
damp and foggy, a fog floated above the trees
white
a white morning
the tops of the trees, the roofs had disappeared
the fog was really thick up there
I wasn't going to take any pictures that day
I'd have to find something else to do now that I wasn't going to work
I had no intention of going to work
that day or maybe ever again
to hell with it! I never liked it
I saw no point in it and now that I wasn't myself I saw even less
that woman—she could go earn her own daily bread to butter
I was through
I was never one of those people who defined himself by what he does for
    a living, no
maybe that's what went wrong, I didn't have that prop

if I had liked my job, if I had thought it was important I could have kept
     going no matter what
habit would have carried me there and back
my whatever—my self could have dissolved, washed away
like dirt or sand
washed away in the rain and left the props, the
frame, the
or—say like an old umbrella somebody tosses
it sits in the weeds, the bushes
after a while the fabric, whatever, rots away until there's nothing left but
     the struts
I could have been like that umbrella if my job had meant something to
     me
if my wife had
meant something
apparently she didn't
it didn't
nothing did apparently
the cat, the kids

    *(Silence)*
I walked around
I went and stood at the newspaper stand and looked at the headlines
they didn't interest me, they didn't concern me
they had nothing to do with me
I was never a political person

And all the time the fog was getting thicker
and lower

What to do?

I started walking home
where my things were, my books and bottles
my camera equipment
went down the street and round the corner and
nothing
it was gone

The fog was sitting there where the house should have been
I felt around in it

nothing, nothing
not a sign, not a clue
just a vacant lot full of trash, old plumbing, and a tub
an old-fashioned tub with feet

(*Silence*)
I've made an assumption
I'm assuming there's somebody here besides me
that I haven't been talking to myself all this time
that, uh, I'm in a room a
an enclosed something—a space
a room
and that I'm not alone
or
if I am
alone
then somebody is watching me
over a TV monitor
or listening to me over a radio
or something
the alternative is too terrible

(*Silence as he listens intently*)
You're very quiet

As I was walking the streets looking for my house, a car passed by
my car
and sitting inside were my wife and kids
wife in the front seat, kids in the back, and next to my wife a man
a complete stranger, I'd never seen him before
I had the feeling that he had replaced me
that he'd somehow
somehow
what?
filled up the place that
that when the world opened up and swallowed me several mornings ago
I was
reconstituted, my molecules or
atoms—juices? something
mutated
in a flash, the blinking of an eye

in the space between the syllables of a single word
I was out and he was in
he was me and I was
I didn't know who

I started to follow the car
took a few steps in the direction it had gone
but where would it get me? what was the point?
and then it, too, disappeared in the fog

I stood there in silence
before moving on

Inside the silence was a tiny sound, a
hum, a
like a ringing in your ears
the world sounded very far away
because of the fog maybe, faint and far off
as if heard through a sickness
the fog wrapped itself around me
all the white morning wrapped me

    *(Silence)*
I remember dreaming that night
several dreams
very vivid
I've been wondering if that's when it happened
I changed
something happened—why not a dream?
In one of them—I assume it was a dream
it may have been real I suppose although it's unlikely
isn't it?
I was sleeping, I woke
sitting on a chair by the bed was an old man
he didn't speak
just sat there smoking cigarettes
an old man with white hair
looking at the floor and smoking silently
I knew he was God
don't ask me how
it was dark in the room

a dark night outside the window
but there was a little light on the floor
around the chair where he sat
which made me think it was he

Who else could it have been, shedding a ring of light?

I didn't notice what brand he was smoking

I fell asleep again

Or dreamed it
and when I woke it was light out and in the room
and he was gone

Odd, the chair was there where he'd sat and looked at the floor
I might have put it there myself
I don't remember
I might have
I moved it back under the desk where it belonged
I went back and looked at the floor again
for, I don't know
evidence
a ring on the wood left by the light
ash
I found nothing
the floor was clean and unmarked
If it weren't for the chair
I might have put it there myself for some reason known only to drunks
I shook it off and went downstairs to breakfast neglecting as you know to
    change out of my pajamas and shave

2.

To continue

There's
how can I explain?
Inside I'm becoming *raw*
do you understand raw?
As if I'd been scraped

my insides
scraped clean with a knife
or as if I'd swallowed ground glass
yes, that's more what I mean
ground-up glass
swallowed
I hurt inside
you picture thousands of tiny cuts
red wounds
sensitive linings
membranes
fissures
red and oozing
not a pretty picture
better not talk about it

But what I want to say is it's strange now that I'm lost I should feel all this
be so sensitive
I never suffered in my life
a twinge here and there
in the teeth, headache
a touch of arthritis, neuralgia
the usual aches and pains
nothing major, not what I'm feeling now
it's as if the
the thing that's gone
call it what you like
got torn out, extracted
like a tooth from the gum or
when they knock a building down
a skyscraper
after they've hauled away the debris
nothing's left except the hole

I had hoped—thought, I'd thought to feel nothing at all under the ci
cumstances
that there would be nothing to feel, no pain when no self, no person to
feel

I was wrong
like a fish, a single-celled organism feels

or a plant winding towards light feels I feel
I was wrong
you can't get rid of it, feeling
it lies coiled in the skin, the cell
a thin ribbon of steel
waiting to rend

They drove off into the fog and I haven't seen them since

I was taken into custody a little while later
I didn't exactly see them
the ones who grabbed me, I
they grabbed me from behind
I never heard them coming
they must have been hiding in the fog
or lost in it
they put a bag over my head, a sack
a rough
burlap
it smelled like onions, an old onion sack maybe
they put it over my head and tied a rope lightly round my neck to keep it
    from coming off
I felt panic

Because of the sack more than anything
it was difficult to breathe through the burlap
the onion smell
not entirely dark, not black
I could see light
dimly
they treated me roughly
although they were careful not to strangle me with the rope—that gave
    me hope
they pushed me along the sidewalk
into a car
shoved me into the back seat, I fell onto the floor
someone got in beside me, the door
slammed
the car
started
nobody said a word

we drove for a while
nobody spoke
the whole time I was on the floor
lying on the side of my face
light flickered through the burlap
we must have been going under bridges or maybe through woods, the
    light flickering through the trees
no one made a sound
the car hummed
the floor was hot against my face
finally it stopped

Once inside, somebody went through my pockets
still not a word
looking for—what, papers
my identity papers?
I had none
I was in my raincoat and pajamas
besides, I had lost it
I was certain I no longer resembled in the slightest any picture of me
    taken before my, my
transformation if that's what it is
but why should God wish me to be transformed
assuming the old man who came and sat by my bed
a chainsmoker
was he, the ancient of days?

Unless it's a fulfillment of the promise, the
prophesy that we
one day, one day to come
we're to be made over
like new
given a new identity

If so, what's mine
and is that why I've been brought here
to receive it?

Or has one thing nothing to do with the other?
have they brought me here because I was seen wandering around in a fog
    in my pajamas

just another vagrant
which I've become
having no home
having mysteriously lost my house?

That stranger who drove away with my wife and kids, he might not have
    been a stranger at all, but me
the me I used to be
who is now changed
beyond recognition
a stranger in fact to all shreds of his former self
that skin

I don't know
it's possible I suppose it's possible
most things are
in the infinitely complicated scheme of things
possible
as we've seen
as history teaches
not to mention our own experience which they say, they're always telling
    us
is the best teacher

Since then, nothing
not a word, not a sound
perhaps
no, I was going to say maybe they don't speak my language but that
    wouldn't have silenced them
it would have emphasized my isolation, my
incomprehension
I wonder
I wonder what's worse
the effect, I mean, on me
this silence
or if they spoke in a language I don't understand
as if I were a text undergoing translation
which in the long run the most harmful?

Assuming they aren't dumb

Unlikely
unlikely to be waylaid by a gang of mutes
a religious order sworn to silence
for what reason?
for a reason to be revealed in time
God's own?


I think the answer lies in something more mundane, more commonplace
    inclining towards my earliest speculations that I was taken into custody
    for loitering in my pajamas, on a public street, with no visible means of
    support, no place of residence
in the visible universe anyway
with a camera
suspicious
that was confiscated and
I assume
opened
in a dark room
its tightly furled secrets prodded
poked
poked and prodded with a fat finger belonging to some functionary of
    whatever's responsible for having me detained


What was on that roll, I wonder
what pictures?


3.


I've been trying to remember what was on the roll
what pictures I had taken


If God had been in my room, what effect did he have on the film, I
    wonder?
God is light, at which end of the spectrum does he exist?
Is he visible light or invisible?
Invisible surely—then how did I see him?
Does he emit x-rays or ultraviolet?
Can he penetrate the closed eyelids, those curtains of blood?
Can you see him if you wear special glasses like the kind you put on at
    a 3-D movie?
What about infrared? would they see him through their instruments,

stumbling across the battlefield at night?
Maybe he's fogged the film
ghosted it
maybe when they develop it they'll see his face but won't recognize it
    through the cigarette smoke
who knows?
Not me
I haven't a clue, not a
there may be nothing there at all
nothing to see at all
an overexposure
just the blackened negative, the empty white print
the nothing that comes from too much light
burned by an excess of light
the radiance
his
heavenly brightness
burning out the film
turning it opaque
impenetrable
so that the print, the white paper print, can't take the imprint finally of the
    light shining through the enlarger
in the last stage
obscures it
arrests it, the light, so that there is no image
nothing
nothing to see
nothing there
nothing at all

Which proves nothing about God's existence one way or the other

    *(Pause)*
I only hope there's nothing incriminating on the roll, nothing
damning
although what that might be I can't imagine, being innocent
a perfectly innocent amateur photographer
family photos
the wife and kids
the house, backyard, the car, the cat
all of it gone

vanished in the fog
snapshots

*(An anguished cry, finally)*
What am I doing here?

4.

It only goes to show it's dangerous to lose your identity
you can replace your passport, your papers
your collection of family photos
if you've had the foresight to store the negatives in another
    place, in case of fire or theft
otherwise, they are irreplaceable
those images you
you'll have to start again taking new pictures
or with a new family
starting your life over
sometimes it's easier that way
easier to begin a new life than to cry inconsolably over the loss of a lot of
    old pictures
but your identity, that's another story
there's nothing you can do
when it's gone it's gone
you just have to wait for it to come back
and if it doesn't, well
there's little you can do about it
practically nothing
except wait

There's no master you, no template
no negative you can store in another place and use to reproduce yourself
and as to going out and starting over, well
it's not that easy, is it?
starting over, not easy to set yourself up somewhere else
because you're empty, you've been emptied out
voided
empty
with nothing to go on
nothing that you might use to reconstruct even a rudimentary self

It's not the same as amnesia where you don't even know your name or
    whether you have a wife, children, a car, a house, a cat
when everything's been erased you can start fresh, let people and events
    write all over you
sooner or later you'll remember who you are or become somebody new
but this, I've been left words, my name, pictures in my head of wife,
    children, car, house and cat, can see them all here in the dark so
so it won't be easy to build over top of them
as if they had never been
even though they might not recognize me if they saw me, so changed am
    I though in what way changed I'm still not sure I understand

Close your eyes and listen
I'm a voice coming at you in the dark
close your eyes
all black
my world
behind the blindfold
black and empty
the world has fallen away, I
afraid
that
later
later they'll come
stub out cigarettes on my skin
put wires into my ears
shove hot wires up
in
beat me with iron rods
beat me

Sometimes I feel something terrible hovering close to me
it beats against my cheek like a wing, why have they brought me here?

When I'm released
if I am
to where
where released and into what when they finally let me go
if they do
if they do
where will I be then?

## 5

Where I am, what's it like?
I haven't seen it
I haven't run my hands over the walls
if there are any walls
I may not be in the narrow space I imagine but in a public square, a
    compound, a dark and endless plain
though there is no wind, no sound, too silent for out of doors
a gymnasium or some vast hall,
an auditorium,
a courtroom sitting bound and blindfolded before silent judges

*(Angry shout)*
Is anyone there?

I can't stand much more of this, how do they expect me to stand this
silent treatment?
I'm confused
I can't get a clear picture of where I am
what they could possibly want from me
am I in a hole, is that it
a hole, a well
the well of despair?

I'm beginning to fall apart
I'm beginning to
I

*(Silence)*
I had a skin condition once
eczema
the skin began to flake from around my nose, my eyes, my eyelids, the
    corners of my mouth—flaked, fell away
I was afraid it would go right on flaking down to the bone
little by little
until the bone, my skull showed through, a skull
of course there was no danger of that happening
still every morning when I woke a new layer of dried skin had peeled
    away during the night and was left hanging in shreds from my face

ready to be sloughed off into the washrag
my morning ablutions, washing away skin, an
erosion
an erasure
I was being slowly erased by my own hand

6.

I want to talk about photography
what I like about it is its fixity
that you can fix someone, a face, a scene
an image, arrest it, stop it from changing
only photography can do that
and death, death can do it, too, except it's more complicated, for the
    person being fixed by death, because the process of disintegration does
    change the dead
what doesn't change is our image of them
the mental picture I'm talking about stays with us
for a long time anyway
for a long time when we think about someone who has died the picture
    we have of him or her is how we last saw him or her alive
but of course the person who dies changes beyond recognition

I took pictures of everything!

Something else that's interesting
it has to do with pictures
is the way pictures—printed pictures turn blue in the sun
you've seen that before, haven't you? how pictures hung in store windows
    after a while they turn blue?
At my wife's hairdresser's I watched the faces of women in the window
photographs illustrating different hairstyles
beautiful women, achingly beautiful if you know what I mean
women rarely seen in nature, models of a perfection that is not of this
    world
our world anyway
I'd watch them from the sidewalk as I stood outside waiting
for my wife to be made over
        (A short laugh)
watched them month after month turn blue as the sun stripped away—
    first the yellow, it's weak and the first to disappear, then the magenta,
        then the black, leaving just the blue, the blue girls looking as if

they'd drowned
or taken cyanide
the beautiful drowned girls floating behind the window
vanishing in sudden reflections of the street
fading like a memory

But photographs never fade
at least not for several lifetimes
which is long enough

Am I dreaming? I may be dreaming

I should have been a professional photographer and sifted life a bit at a
    time, frame by frame, photo by photo
better than a librarian
writing's of no use to anyone
stories
no one cares anymore
it hasn't anything to do with anything
life
life on a page
marks on a page, the one has nothing at all to do with the other
just words
pictures lie closer to what's visible and what's not visible can't be
    rendered
except in dreams
and as soon as you put a dream to paper it loses its reality
or unreality
it isn't convincing any longer

If someone were to take my picture now would I be a blank
a nothing
air
not even smoke
just thin air?

My happiest times were spent in the darkroom
there I was in control
and it is so restful
the dark
so easy on the eyes, so

and the way a face, a scene
life composes itself at the bottom of the developer bath
emerges under the red light
and is fixed there
so that not even death can alter it

In the dark
the silent room
not a soul around
just images blooming indelibly at the bottom of the tray
underwater
wavering like the faces of the drowned
in the bath
sprawling pastures, meadows dotted with flowers quietly submerged in
    the bath
mountains ringed by flood
streets and houses
faces smiling up at me from their watery grave

What does it mean to be dead?

On the subject of death all the experts are silent

Still
you ought to be able to guess
have an informed opinion
informed by what you've experienced in living
life being, as we are told, a mere preparation
an exercise for death
only less so

Is that what this is
an exercise?

Or am I dead?

The day I was born someone went to the store and bought a gun
a high-powered rifle with sharpshooter's scope
it sat in the closet or on a shelf
until on another day
the day I got married maybe

a beautiful day as I remember
he went to the store and bought a box of bullets
beautiful in their brass jackets
now he is driving toward the outskirts of town
the light flickers over his hands as he drives under the trees
now he is walking through the woods
he's in no hurry, he's early, he'll have plenty of time
he carries the rifle cradled in his arms
the weight of the bullets makes the pocket of his hunting jacket sag
soon he will walk into the clearing
he's early, he has time to smoke a cigarette
listen to the birds
the wind in the trees
they're bringing me to him as if to a wedding

A marriage
arranged the day I was born
he's been waiting patiently all these years
the day has come
the bullets fit the gun perfectly
they're made for each other
we're made for each other
there's not the slightest doubt that this is what I was born to do
all of us
there's a bullet waiting for all of us
it's got our name on it, yours and mine
no matter if we change our name, change our identity, we can't change
    that
our destiny
which is death
in an open clearing
or an enclosed space
the jumping off point between this world and the next

If there is
if there is

7.

I'm dividing
what's left is

breaking up
coming apart
dissolving
into bits
atoms
bits
particles of consciousness I
I'm in the river and the water tears at me
the water floods me
the water is eating me away
where's my mind going?
I'm disappearing
I can feel the life running out of me like sand
I'm being airbrushed out

8.

Disappeared
I—no
no I, no me
disappeared
gone

9.

    (Silence)
I imagine my own death
I imagine it more strongly than I have ever done
I am walking the beach
it is late afternoon and the light is falling
I take a gun from my pocket
I can feel the ring of the barrel hard and cold against my forehead
I'll fire and fall face down in the water after I fire, I won't know anything
    more
I see myself lying face down in the water with my feet in the wet sand
the waves roll over me, tug each time at the wound
they suck the blood little by little from my forehead until I'm white
white as a ghost

When I was a kid I used to have nightmares
I'd wake in the middle of the night, shaking

once my mother came into my room and found me trembling
I told her about my nightmares
she said she could suck them out of my head so that I wouldn't have them
    anymore
every night before I went to sleep she'd come into my room and suck my
forehead
I didn't have them after that
not for a long time anyway
not till now
now that there's no one to suck them out

I imagine myself lying face down while the water sucks my head clean of
    nightmares
no more bad dreams ever again
unless you dream in the ground
do you dream when you're dead and if you do, what do you dream?

Of worms singing in your ears
and what do the worms sing?

Something shrill and terrible

No more talk about death
no more

10.

Today someone brought me water
he didn't say anything
still, I'm not forgotten
someone brought me water
the cup at my lip—I expected vinegar
or urine
"I'm not political," I said
he didn't answer
they must know that
that I'm not political
it was water, plain water, it had gone flat, but it was water
he said nothing
I smelled him
his sweat, his smell

something he'd just eaten was on his breath
meat
liquor
he gave me water

My expectations are high
I haven't been forgotten
I'm not political
they must have examined the photographs
innocent scenes
apolitical
they could not have interpreted them any other way
pictures of my wife, the kids, the cat, the house
street scenes, scenes of the countryside
all innocent all
banal
a waste of film
my expectations are high
soon perhaps I'll be fed
they know now that I'm not political
I've been watered, soon I hope to be fed
and then my hands
untied
the blindfold
removed
I've been forgiven

Perhaps my new identity is being readied now
my new papers, my
prints, a new face
some new I I've never yet imagined
I'll leave here a new man
soon
if not today
tomorrow
if not tomorrow, the day after

II.

It's not so bad
this is not so bad, it's not so bad here

it could be worse
I haven't been beaten
I expected to be beaten
I haven't been abused
no one has hurt me
no one has touched me
spat at me, reviled me
hurt me
I wish someone would touch me
not hurt, just touch, the slightest pressure

A hand grazing mine
a finger
a hand, a finger—something to interrupt this weightlessness, this
    loneliness
to be beaten would be something anyway
to be hurt
not hurt too much but
a little
a small hurt to let me know I'm not living among ghosts

To be given water isn't enough
to be given food isn't enough

To be spoken to

A voice in the dark

A voice to come out of the dark
at me

Into me

A voice would be enough

12.

I am waiting for the earth to give up its dead
I am waiting for them to shake off their coats of clay
of dust
of indifference

I am waiting for them to shake off sleep
I'm with them
the apolitical dead
I am with them under the ground
our final resting place
our common ground
I'm waiting for them to come and embrace me
wind their bony fingers in my hair
dissolve my bonds, my body, my bounds
lead me to where we all dance the last ecstatic dance
waiting for the roof to be pried off and for whatever it is that is outside to
    spill in like water
like blood
like light

I see them now
they are bruised with shadow
they bear the marks of their torture
they are silent, they've lost their tongues
pink erasers, their tongues lie quietly in desk drawers
everything is a blank
documents
passports
papers—everything has been erased
the words have scuttled from the pages of books leaving them empty
the words have crawled into the corners, into the shadows in the corners
    of the room, into the sprawling dark
the dead are approaching slowly with their slender means

Someone's coming
the dead flinch back into shadow
press themselves against walls
jibber unintelligibly that they have no politics
he's coming to lay the black pill of silence on my tongue
he will show me the instruments
he will instruct me in pain
he is coming for me with his radiant knife
to cut out my tongue

I know who I am
I know it now

I will root here
my skin will whiten
my bones will dissolve and my skin become loathsome
my body will become a finger
a thing belonging to the dark
fingering the earth
blind urgency in the dry earth
making a place in the belly of the ground
listening without ears to the dirt give way
a vein in the earth waiting to be stripped out

I know what I am
a thing belonging to the dark
a root
my new identity
sleep
the long vegetable sleep
then dirt
then stone and the sleep of stone
then stone
then nothing  ✧

**FICTION**  POST ROAD

# The Ciné

Barry Gifford

On a cloudy October Saturday in 1953, when Roy was seven years old, his father took him to see a movie at the Ciné theater on Bukivona Avenue in Chicago, where they lived. Roy's father drove them in his powder-blue Cadillac, bumping over cobblestones and streetcar tracks, until he parked the car half a block from the theater.

Roy was wearing a brown-and-white-checked wool sweater, khaki trousers, and saddle shoes. His father wore a double-breasted blue suit with a white silk tie. They held hands as they walked towards the Ciné. The air was becoming colder every day now, Roy noticed, and he was eager to get inside the theater, to be away from the wind. The Ciné sign had a red background over which the letters curved vertically in yellow neon. They snaked into one another like reticulate pythons threaded through branches of a thick-trunked Cambodian bo tree. The marquee advertised the movie they were going to see, *King of the Khyber Rifles*, starring Tyrone Power as King, a half-caste British officer commanding Indian cavalry riding against Afghan and other insurgents. "Tyrone Cupcake," Roy's father called him, but Roy did not know why.

Roy and his father entered the Ciné lobby and headed for the concession stand, where Roy's father bought Roy buttered popcorn, a Holloway All-Day sucker, and a Dad's root beer. Inside the cinema, they chose seats fairly close to the screen on the right-hand side. The audience was composed mostly of kids, many of whom ran up and down the aisles even during the show, shouting and laughing, falling and spilling popcorn and drinks.

The movie began soon after Roy and his father were in their seats, and as Tyrone Power was reviewing his mounted troops, Roy's father whispered to his son, "The Afghans were making money off the opium trade even back then."

"What's opium, Dad," asked Roy.

"Hop made from poppies. The Afghans grow and sell them to dope dealers in other countries. Opium makes people very sick."

"Do people eat it?"

"They can, but mostly they smoke it and dream."

"Do they have bad dreams?"

"Probably bad and good. Users get ga-ga on the pipe. Once somebody's hooked on O, he's finished as a man."

"What about women? Do they smoke it, too?"

"Sure, son. Only Orientals, though, that I know of. Sailors in Shanghai, Hong Kong, Zamboanga, get on the stem and never make it back to civilization."

"Where's Zamboanga?"

"On Mindanao, in the Phillipine Islands."

"Is that a long way from India and Afghanistan?"

"Every place out there is a long way from everywhere else."

"Can't the Khyber Rifles stop the Afghans?"

"Tyrone Cupcake'll kick 'em in the pants if they don't."

Roy and his father watched Tyrone Power wrangle his minions for about twenty minutes before Roy's father whispered in Roy's ear again.

"Son, I've got to take care of something. I'll be back in a little while. Before the movie's over. Here's a dollar," he said, sticking a bill into Roy's hand, "just in case you want more popcorn."

"Dad," said Roy, "don't you want to see what happens?"

"You'll tell me later. Enjoy the movie, son. Wait for me here."

Before Roy could say anything else, his father was gone.

The movie ended, and Roy's father had not returned. Roy remained in his seat while the lights were on. He had eaten the popcorn and drunk his root beer, but he had not yet unwrapped the Holloway All-Day sucker. People left the theater and other people came in and took their seats. The movie began again.

Roy had to pee badly, but he did not want to leave his seat in case his father came back while he was in the men's room. Roy held it until he could not any longer and then allowed a ribbon of urine to trickle down his left pantsleg into his sock and onto the floor. The chair on his left, where his father had been sitting, was empty, and an old lady seated on his right did not seem to notice that Roy had urinated. The odor was covered up by the smell of popcorn, candy, and cigarettes.

Roy sat in his wet trousers, and soaked left sock and shoe, watching again as Captain King exhorted his Khyber Rifles to perform heroically. This time after the film was finished, Roy got up and walked out with the rest of the audience. He stood under the theater marquee and waited for his father. It felt good to Roy to be out of the close, smoky cinema now. The sky was dark, just past dusk, and the people filing into the Ciné were mostly couples on Saturday night dates.

Roy was getting hungry. He took out the Holloway All-Day, unwrapped it, and took a lick. A uniformed policeman came and stood near him. Roy was not tempted to say anything about his situation to the beat cop because he remembered his father saying to him more than once, "The police are not your friends." The police officer looked once at Roy, smiled at him, then moved away.

Roy's mother was in Cincinnati, visiting her sister, Roy's Aunt Theresa. Roy decided to walk to where his father had parked, to see if his powder-blue Cadillac was still there. Maybe his father had gone wherever he had gone on foot, or taken a taxi. A black-and-gold-trimmed

Studebaker Hawk was parked where Roy's father's car had been.

Roy returned to the Ciné. The policeman who had smiled at him was standing again in front of the theater. Roy passed by without looking at the cop, licking his Holloway All-Day. His left pantsleg felt crusty but almost dry, and his sock still felt soggy. The cold wind made Roy shiver, and he rubbed his arms. A car horn honked. Roy turned and saw the powder-blue Caddy stopped in the street. His father was waving at him out the driver's side window.

Roy walked to and around the front of the car, opened the passenger side door, and climbed in, pulling the heavy metal door closed. Roy looked out the window at the cop standing in front of the Ciné: one of his hands rested on the butt of his holstered pistol and the other fingered the grooves on the handle of his billy club as his eyes swept the street.

"Sorry I'm late, son," Roy's father said. "Took me a little longer than I thought it would. Happens sometimes. How was the movie? Did Ty Cupcake take care of business?" ✧

# Scar

Robert Lopez

This Deborah talks out of the left side of her mouth, as if she's trying to keep what she says secret from her own right ear. She wears three or four earrings in each one. Two hoops of equal size and little silver balls that trail up her lobes like tracks.

I see the tracheotomy scar immediately. She leaves the top two buttons of her blouse undone like she's saying, Here I am, beaten and scarred, take it or leave it.

I've decided not to say anything, pretending either not to notice or care. Whichever she decides.

She talks a lot out of the left side of her mouth, which is good. The little I say I'm tired of hearing myself say it. And this Deborah doesn't seem to care one way or the other, which is even better. Match made in heaven.

Just as we are pulling up to a red light she says like she is accusing me of something, You're not wearing the seat belt. I answer I only put it on when it rains. Out of the left side of her mouth comes, You've never gone through the windshield.

There are only a few cars on this road to wherever it is we're going. Some exotic barbeque place well off the beaten path. She spends most of the ride going through her purse like she is looking for something. She pretends to be preoccupied most of the time, I think. Otherwise she *is* preoccupied most of the time and I'm making her out to be clever in a way she isn't. I turn the radio on and scan the stations, pretending that finding a good song is important to me. She stops going through her purse without having pulled anything out of it.

I don't know whether or not she is expecting me to defend myself, my position on car safety. I just keep going up and down the dial, pausing to hear the end of a Willie Nelson song and most of "It's All Right" by the Impressions.

Because I don't have a lot to say people tell me I'm a good listener. But I don't think that's right, either.

I haven't gone through a windshield, never even come close. I've never been injured or seen anyone seriously injured. I was at a party once as a teenager where someone was killed in a backyard brawl but it happened after I had left. He got his shoulder or his neck slashed with a beer bottle and bled to death.

All during dinner I try to imagine this Deborah going through the windshield, the mechanics of it, what actually happens when one goes through the windshield. I try to see her head making contact with the glass and shattering it. I try to see her body careening off the hood and landing on the concrete.

The thing is she doesn't look like someone who'd gone through a windshield. If anything she looks like someone who'd been robbed at gunpoint, maybe assaulted. (One of those women that takes a self-defense class and carries a gun afterwards.) Nothing where she was hanging on by a thread, hooked up to machines with one foot in the grave. I'm just guessing about that part, but it stands to reason.

She wears a lot of makeup but not enough to cover up any facial scars. She flaunts the one on her neck like it's a piece of jewelry.

We go back to her place, which has two bedrooms and hardwood floors. On the ride over I fastened the seat belt but I don't think she noticed. She opened her purse but didn't go through it like she did before, probably just making sure the gun was loaded and accessible.

This Deborah's hair is thick, more or less straight and dry to the touch. There's a spot on the back of her calf that's irritated from shaving. I think her left leg might be longer than the right leg but that could just be my imagination making her more interesting. The feet are bony so I leave them alone. Stomach needs work. I'm guessing the nipples aren't sensitive because she seems bored when I work them.

I try to decide if she reminds me of someone.

I don't know what she sees in me, if anything. My body is smooth and unbroken. No runs, no hits, no errors. I don't have anything to say and though I listen to people when they talk, I don't know if that makes me good at it.

She searches me up and down, says, I'm exploring you. Who knows what she is looking for but her exploration feels good, so I let her explore me. I tell her to let me know if she finds anything worthwhile. For what-ever reason the line, Close your eyes and think of England, comes to me. I am Queen Victoria or whoever it was with my eyes closed and she is Magellan in search of god knows what.

She pushes her tongue against mine like she's angry at it. The sound she makes is between a moan and a sigh. Every so often she pulls back and has a playful grin on her face. Eventually I start mimicking her, so that each time our lips are about to touch I pull back.

She smiles, tells me out of the left side of her mouth that I'm the first one to pass her test.

I say, I guess you've met your match.

I start behind the ear. She makes her sound and grabs hold of the back of my head, digging her nails into my scalp. Eventually I get to where we both want this to go. I run my tongue back and forth over the spot. The skin feels dead. ✧

# Hot Waters

Paul Eberly

**D**riving west of Pueblo, Jennifer and Mack were talking about masturbation. It was a game of confessions. She left the office during lunch to please herself in their Volvo wagon. He spent weeks in the field and consoled himself in pensions, alone on meager beds. To admit this was embarrassing but titillating. "Do you look at magazines while you do it?" she asked. "*Playboy,* or what's the other one, *Penthouse?* Do they have those in Sumatra?"

"No," Mack fibbed, "I only think of you."

U.S. 50 described a serpentine through the Colorado Rockies. The Volvo hummed dependably. They'd bought the vehicle in anticipation of children, before she knew of her wrecked uterus, before he knew his sperm were lassitudinous and rare.

"I don't enjoy it," he told her, truthfully this time. "It feels medicinal. It reminds me you're not with me."

"I can't say I have that problem. For me, it always feels good." She glanced consolingly at him. "I hope you're not hurt.

"I don't do it a lot," she added. "I don't get horny like you."

On the steering wheel, her fingers were tapered, and under her denims, her thigh muscles shifted as she worked the pedals. He imagined her in the parking lot outside her office tower, imagined the tapered skirt of one of her severe suits, hiked around her hips. Ahead, a snow-dusted ranch road intersected the highway, ran south, then disappeared between outcrops of buff-colored stone. His chest felt vacant. "I'd love to watch you," he said. "I mean, could I?" He pointed toward the rock mounds. "There's a hidden spot there."

Suddenly, he noticed, the flesh appeared slacker around her jaw and pouches materialized under her eyelids. This had begun to happen—her age would flicker across her features like heat lightning. He could see her mood had cratered. "What is it?" he said.

She shook her head. They lit cigarettes.

"Come on," he said, "talk to me." Sometimes, if he acted quickly, he could turn her attitude around before it really plummeted. Her moods were sharp but transient, while his were cloying and savage. And her moods could trigger his. He worked to buoy her as a measure of self-defense.

The car filled with smoke. The ranch road receded. "I remembered something," she said.

"What?"

"I remembered how we pestered Doctor Thibodaux to let us have sex after we found out I was pregnant." A tear tracked over her cheek-bone, and her pores looked wider. "We should have waited."

"We did not pester him. We asked, and he said we could do it. Whatever killed the embryo, it wasn't our making love."

"We did pester him. I remember. And he hesitated. The books say you should wait three months with problem pregnancies. And if anyone had a problem pregnancy, I did."

Gloom invaded Mack, settling in his chest. There'd been a time when they'd talked of little but their failure to make a child, but Jennifer had gotten resistant to the topic. They'd barely broached it these last three years. So it surprised him, her resurrecting it now. The road ascended into saw-tooth mountains, and he stayed sunk into himself as they climbed. She laid her hand on his thigh. "I'm sorry," she said. "Leave home, things pop out. I suppose it was talking about sex that made me think of it. Sometimes it ambushes me. Can we turn this around?"

It ambushed him regularly. He'd forget for a day, even a week, but those events would reinsinuate themselves, awaking with him in the morning, riding shotgun as he drove to the school. Now, he studied the back seat. The upholstery was crumb-free and unstained. By rights, the seat should be a wreck, sticky with residue of upended Happy Meals, disfigured by colored markers. "I guess that was my fault, too," he said. "If I hadn't been whining for sex, we wouldn't have asked him."

Maybe their lovemaking had killed the embryo, but he rarely thought of that first IVF. Instead, he thought of their second try, when the embryos didn't implant. Then, Thibodaux hadn't liked Jennifer's egg quality, and he liked the resulting embryos less. He liked her uterine lining least of all. As he injected the embryos, his pessimism expressed itself in a grimace only Mack could see. After the transfer, he sent them home, prescribing for Jennifer two days in bed.

Leaving the clinic, Mack drove gingerly, not to jar her. After settling her on the fold-out with a stack of videotapes, he climbed the stairs to his home office, a room they planned to use as a nursery. He needed to finish a proceedings paper, a revised taxonomy for the bats of Sumatra, and the manuscript was due in twenty-four hours. He worked. He didn't ask himself how the dog got inside, or who fed the VCR with fresh cassettes.

The paper went terribly. And he felt stung by a peculiar fatigue. They'd spent years in labs and clinics. He'd ignored his research until, it seemed to him, the other faculty began to treat him like a plague victim. He didn't believe this attempt would work. Clearly, Thibodaux didn't either. At the same time, and oddly, he found it hard to think they could fail. Each time Mack checked, Jennifer appeared angrier. By ten, she'd gotten icy and withdrawn.

"Talk," he said. "What's the problem?"

"You're supposed to be taking *care* of me!"

"I am taking care of you. I'm trying to make tenure." He sat on the edge of the mattress. "The paper's going like shit, and it's due tomorrow."

"The fucking paper," she said. "*Fuck* the paper." She winged the remote at the television; it hit with a cracking sound. Mack was surprised the screen didn't break. Jennifer started to weep. "My God," she said. "I'm supposed to stay calm."

He blotted her cheeks with Kleenex, then held her and kissed her brow. He rubbed her feet and brewed her herbal tea. The next day, he disassembled the computer and carried it to the dining room to be near her. By afternoon, he decided he'd miss his deadline. He'd struggled through Ph.D. and Post Doc, landed a gig at a top school, to jeopardize it in this monomaniacal quest for kids. He'd caught malaria, chasing his bats. Why, when they'd understood the strikes against them, couldn't they surrender? He could have. This obsession—Jennifer's—was unseemly.

He knew his surliness affected her, but Jennifer's fixation on staying calm, which she shared with Thibodaux, seemed like New Age bullshit. As if the human constitution were so precarious. Women got pregnant in war zones, they got pregnant during famines. At ten after five he printed the manuscript. In the family room, he fit the paper into the fax machine without checking for typos. It was after seven on the East Coast—there, the deadline was two hours gone. He keyed the number and pressed Send.

"How's it going?" Jennifer asked timidly.

"Fine," he said. He experienced a desire to quit talking, to let his pulse slow. But something had a hook in him. "I just blew a critical publication. No big matter. It's just another dropped ball—down at the Department, I'm ankle deep in them. The faculty will pelt me with them when I go for tenure."

Her cheeks looked fragile as tissue. "Please..." she said. Her voice was barely audible.

He smiled, he realized, nastily. "Hey," he said. "I'm not worried. I can always teach high school. I'll find something to pay the bills. What do you care, as long as you get what you're after?"

"Me?" Jennifer said. "What I'm after?" Her shoulders started to heave as she sobbed in a choking way he'd never seen before. "You asshole," she said. "You're such a fucking asshole." She rolled into a ball, as if she were a fetus. He felt like he'd awoken from a blackout. More than once, *he'd* been the one pushing them forward, when she seemed ready to quit. He climbed onto the mattress and tried to embrace her, but she stayed closed to him.

The paper was published; the embryos didn't implant. The next time they tried, Thibodaux halted the procedure. Jennifer's uterus, he decided, had become too diseased. Of course, Mack received tenure. The faculty seemed surprised he'd considered his status in doubt. But he doubted himself. Why had his capacity for kindness failed at the critical moment? The answers weren't mitigating. And knowing how much he'd wanted a child made it impossible to believe Jennifer would forgive him. Once, he'd kissed a graduate assistant but stopped things before they went further. Another time, he'd claimed false deductions on their 1040. But until that afternoon, he'd never done anything that truly compromised his sense of himself as a decent person. Since then, he'd never thought of himself as truly decent, or good.

A spray of sand hissed against the windshield. The sky looked lifeless, fractured by linear clouds. "Sometimes," he said, "I don't know how we keep living together."

"Could it be we love each other?"

"I let us down," he said. "Remember?"

She hesitated. "I remember. But we don't know that had anything to do with my not getting pregnant."

"Except we'll never be sure, will we?"

"No," she said, "we won't. And we'll never be sure my picking up that planter didn't wreck things either. Remember that?" The planter was an eight-gallon earthenware. Then, as now, it contained a man-sized rubber tree. "I don't know what got into my head. I didn't think. Or I did think. I was tired of fertility treatments determining everything I did."

"That planter didn't have anything to do with it."

"Look," she said. "I've learned this much. There're things it doesn't help talking about. They only make you miserable. Whatever happened that afternoon, I don't understand it and it's not how I see you. But I've put it behind me. You should, too."

They drove in silence, and she pushed an Irving Berlin CD into the player. The music didn't cheer him. He'd run out of cigarettes, so he took one of hers. He felt sickened by his desire of moments earlier to watch her pleasure herself. It had never occurred to him that desire for sex— *his* desire—might have ruined the *first* of their efforts. This was a new twist, one that put him at fault for two failures. Professor Mack, the baby killer. For weeks preceding this trip, he'd imagined they'd spend most of the weekend naked. Now, the idea of lovemaking seemed repulsive.

He brooded till they reached Buena Vista. The town was too small to merit a stoplight. To the east, the mountains were mantled with snow. A sign announced the pass was closed.

"Oh," Jennifer said.

"Don't worry," he said, "the springs are in the foothills."

"Well, I want lunch. And it's afternoon." She slowed as they passed the town's few eateries. "Look, that one's crowded."

"I'm not hungry."

She eyed him sharply. "Will you please come off it? I'm starting to get tired of this. You might want to mope all weekend, but I don't."

In the diner, they ordered salads. Sometimes, as now, he'd find himself infected with the illogical notion that she might actually *be* pregnant—that Thibodaux's efforts had finally taken. Among bats, females could conceive months after mating, the sperm having camped inside them, awaiting the martyrdom of fertilization. It seemed giddily conceivable that the IVF attempts, fraught as they'd been, had left a similar residuum, one that would pounce unexpected, striking them dizzy with pleasure. To ground himself, he studied the other diners.

At the table beside them, a middle-aged couple sat with a boy in his teens. The boy was barely younger than the kids who took Mack's classes. The man wore a Yankees cap; he looked like Mack felt. The woman lacked eyebrows and wore a scarf on her head. Before her sat only a saucer of Jell-O. Clearly, she'd received chemotherapy. She seemed to be having trouble breathing. Mack tapped Jennifer's wrist. "Look," he whispered.

The woman's flesh had taken a bluish tinge, and when she tried to stand, her legs folded so she collapsed into her chair with a painful-sounding thump. Her husband regarded her perplexedly, as if he were staring at a blackboard crowded with quantum physics. The boy addressed him. "She can't make it any higher," he said. He banged his glass on the table; water sloshed onto the varnished wood. "You have to *decide* something." The man shrugged, then squeezed the woman's wrist. He stood and walked to the parking lot. Mack watched him through the window as he opened a cell phone. He stared at the clouds as he spoke into the receiver.

Jennifer knelt by the sick woman. "Let's get her down," she told the boy. Together, they helped her into a supine position, and Jennifer rolled Mack's jacket into a ball, then slipped it under her head. She studied Mack uncertainly. Because he was a mammalian biologist, she always seemed to think he'd possess useful medical knowledge. Helplessly, he shrugged. They each looked toward the boy, hoping for an explanation, but he seemed close to crying, which made him appear younger. He stroked his mother's cheek with the backs of his fingers, as if she were a beloved cat.

The husband returned, and without speaking the four of them made a protective circle around her, Mack and Jennifer holding her ankles, the husband and son taking her hands. Waitresses fussed around them. To Mack, the woman's ankle felt like rawhide-wrapped bone. He thought she regarded her husband with peculiar resentment; the husband, for his part, avoided her gaze. She also awarded Mack a disapproving look, as if he and the husband were jokers drawn from a single deck. She squeezed the son's hand till her knuckles turned white. Each time anyone left, a cold blast pounded through the door, chilling her. She trembled. Surprisingly quickly, it seemed to Mack, a chest-filling *whump whump*

*whump* invaded the room. The sound was familiar from research in Sumatra and Nepal, where helicopters were often the only means of transportation. Through the windows, he watched a Medivac chopper settle in the gravel lot, raising a cyclone of cigarette butts and dust.

Mack and Jennifer were immediately marginalized. The wife, strapped onto a narrow gurney, disappeared into the helicopter, her face obscured by an oxygen mask. The husband and son dashed to a grime-covered SUV, then sped north toward Denver. In minutes, the family had disappeared. "My God," Jennifer said. "We didn't find out their names. We can't even check on them."

The spa was located west of Buena Vista, before the road climbed in earnest. The ground was steely with snow that had softened, then crusted over. Jennifer braked in the driveway, and together they stared, nonplussed. The lodge, a western-style motel, was ill-kept: a pane in the lobby door had been replaced by cardboard, and the window frames were weathered to wood. Four cabins sat in a string above the river. Each was assembled from a hodgepodge of construction materials, so they looked like havens for hillbillies. A pair of oddly beautiful bunnies hopped about the cabin nearest. "Well," Jennifer said, "the cabins are cute."

The lobby was rustic and smelled of vegetarian cooking. The carpet had worn through, revealing the plywood floor. A sign hung above the office window, bearing a glyph composed of stylized arrows that looked to Mack like interlocking sperm cells. The sign read, "The rules of life—love is all there is, do harm to no one, we are all one." Mack rang the bell, and a heavy-set, fifty-ish female appeared, leading a lame retriever. She grinned guilelessly. Her hair was long and streaked with silver, and she wore a tie-dyed top over a long-sleeved, thermal undershirt. This, Mack thought, is what happened to the hippy chicks.

She opened the spa's ledger. "Do you have reservations?" she asked, still cheesing. Mack gave their last names, and she looked puzzled. "That's weird, I don't have you down here." He noticed Jennifer's lips tighten. The hippy chick brightened. "But no matter, I've got a room for you."

Jennifer scanned the lobby doubtfully. "Tell us about the cabins."

"They're wonderful. Each has its own kitchenette and a private spring. They're the only area that's completely clothing-optional."

"Are any available?"

Now, the woman appeared doleful. "Unfortunately, we just had the best come open. There was a couple coming from Denver. She's dying—cancer—and her final wish was to spend a night in the mountains. They were going to stay in Cabin One, that's our honeymoon unit. I guess they got as far as Buena Vista, and she got altitude sick and dehydrated. The husband was so busy putting things together, he forgot to bring water and oxygen. Badabing. Next thing you know, she's in a helicopter."

Jennifer looked like she'd been slapped. "And they were supposed to get *that* cabin?"

The hippy chick nodded. "But now it's open. If you stay in it, I'll ask you to light candles for them. White candles—one, then another. I'll give them to you. To send them some positive energy."

Jennifer squeezed Mack's elbow. "What do you think?"

As naively ridiculous as the idea seemed, that lighting any number of candles could improve the stricken woman's fortunes, Mack felt reluctant. What if they fell asleep and failed to light the second candle? What if he clouded the positive "vibes" with his own dour thoughts? Jennifer clearly wanted to go ahead with it. "Okay," he said, relenting and fishing his credit card from his wallet.

Jennifer said, "How do you *know* all this?"

"I just got off the phone with the husband. The poor schmoe's the kind of dude who takes things hard. At least she got to *look* at the mountains. Hopefully, he'll give himself credit for what he managed and forgive himself for the rest of it. Screwing up only proves he's human."

The cabin was so cold they could see their breaths. It contained a wood stove and a pair of radiant heaters, and Mack plugged the heaters in, then switched them to high. Staying dressed, Jennifer slipped beneath the comforter and flipped through a magazine. Mack settled at the table and opened a journal to an article about rodent pulmonary systems. The candles rested on the dresser. Jennifer read. Mack watched—her contentedness made him disgruntled. He didn't want sex—that was ruined—but he wanted her to want it. This was a woman whose cravings were powerful enough to drive her to the parking lot during work for deliverance. *That* factoid still made him spin. Yet, at last, they were alone, and she seemed prepared to spend the afternoon studying photos of the Queen Mum's funeral.

He walked outside to examine the private spring. It was a man-made, rock-lined bowl, fed by a rusty conduit. To Mack's eye, it didn't appear large enough to accommodate the two of them. In the cold air, the hot water steamed like a witch's brew, smelling mildly of sulfur. The sun had settled behind the trees. Too irked to return to the cabin, Mack wandered to the lodge and examined a bulletin board attached to the lobby wall. Seeing him, the retriever issued a desultory growl. The bulletin board listed the spa's services: past-life regression, massage—watsu and Ayurvedic, and computerized aura analysis. So far, he'd seen only the earth grandma, and he wondered whether she, personally, performed all these services. The dog's tail began to thump, and Mack heard a footfall behind him.

"We're not doing watsu at the present," the hippy woman said. "Too damn cold. But now's a good time for any of the other therapies. Late afternoons are sluggish, you know. Most of the guests are in town, finding dinner."

It occurred to Mack he didn't know the woman's name. He offered his hand. Hers was dry and compact. "My name's Mack," he told her.

He expected she'd tell him her name was Mountain Meadow or something similar, but she shot him that now familiar smile and said, "Call me Gayle." She stepped to his side and studied the corkboard with him, as if she'd never noticed it before. "So what can I do you for?"

Mack didn't want to go back to the cabin, and now that she'd pressed him to decide on a therapy, it would be awkward to refuse. Routinely, he made fun of New Age silliness, but here, hundreds of miles from the University, with Jennifer reading or asleep, who'd know? "What," he said, "*therapy* do you think would help me?"

She inspected him gravely. "I'm not certain," she said. "But you do need something, that's for sure." The grin returned. "Well... aura's usually a good place to start."

The aura analysis station occupied a carrel fashioned of cherry paneling. Inside, a dated PC perched on a battered sideboard. Cables snaked across the floor. At the carrel's center sat a Formica kitchenette with paired vinyl chairs. Gayle nodded toward one, and Mack sat in it, finding himself lens-to-eyeball with a tripod-mounted video camera. She turned on the PC and adjusted the camera's position. "You have to place your hand in the biosensor," she told him. "Slip your fingers into the silver loopty-loops."

A black metal slab the size and shape of a collegiate dictionary rested before Mack; five metal rings projected from the top of it. He felt ridiculous, but he slipped his fingers through them.

"Flatten your palm against the metal," Gayle ordered. "Now it's calibrating."

Mack scrutinized her. Her years and weight notwithstanding, Gayle projected a disheveled, almost feral sensuality. She'd been a hippy chick how many years? Probably thirty or more. He wondered how many lovers she'd had. She was talking. "The camera measures both your video image and your electromagnetic spectrum. Its like those Kirlian cameras Tesla experimented with, except this one's more advanced. As you see, it's computerized—the whole thing's gotten very scientific."

Mack suffered a pang of guilt. Gayle was brimful with enthusiasm. "I don't believe any of this," he said.

She was tapping the keyboard. "That doesn't matter."

Abruptly, Mack's head and shoulders appeared on the monitor. In the image, he was surrounded and suffused by a nimbus of dull colors.

"That couple," Gayle said, "the man and the sick woman? They called a few minutes ago. Apparently, they got her stabilized at the hospital. Now they're on their way back up here, armed with oxygen and extra water. Who knows whether they'll make it? Obviously, she's pretty determined."

Mack recalled the woman's face as she lay on the diner floor—loving yet resentful, resigned yet resolute. "Will they be wanting the cabin?" he said. "We can move into the lodge if that'll help."

"Don't worry, like I said, they might not even make it. She's at death's door—this is a desperation attempt. And I have another cabin ready—number two, right next to you."

"But they wanted the honeymoon cabin—"

"Mack, for them the honeymoon's over. Maybe it never happened. They're saying goodbye now." As she studied the monitor, Gayle's face turned rueful. "Boy oh boy," she said. "Mister, you are some kind of mess!"

"A mess?" Mack repeated dumbly.

"First of all, your colors are muddy. Your primary's yellow—that indicates a tendency to overanalyze, and that you're really hypercritical. All this fuchsia shows an inclination to obsessiveness, that you're intolerant and depressive. And this red—that means you're living in survival mode." Gayle motioned for Mack to rise. "Stand up, so we can image your chakras. But keep your fingers in the rings." On the monitor, balls of light appeared in an irregular line superimposed over a dark silhouette that could or could not have been his. They started above the figure's head and descended to its groin. Gayle pointed to them. "Badabing. Your chakras are the troubling part. In a healthy person, these chakra positions ought to look like flowers on a plumb bob, all in a line. Except, look—yours are all cattywhompus. What's really scary's your heart chakra." In the center of the figure's chest glowed a tiny sun. It was red as an ember. "That muddy red heart chakra proves all this negative energy's self-directed. Mister Man, you're plenty pissed at yourself. There's something eating you. You need to soak, soak, soak in our healing waters."

Mack's brain felt adrift, like it was floating in salad oil. Once, Jennifer's youngest cousin, a pretty but aloof twenty-something who'd spent years following the Grateful Dead, had thrown the Tarot for him. The cards were disturbingly on the mark. This sensation was the same as the one he'd experienced then, except magnified many times over. He slipped his fingers free of the biosensor and started for the door, stumbling over loose cables. As he passed, Gayle shied from him, as if she feared his malign electromagnetics might infect her.

Outside, the wind had kicked up, and it plucked Mack's clothing as he crossed to the cabin. The temperature felt thirty degrees lower. He hurried, trying not to think about his unhappy aural health. Somewhere, Jennifer had found firewood, and she'd built a fire in the stove. She'd undressed. The flames cast a fluttery glow across her belly and high, small breasts. Unwillingly, he began to respond to her.

"I want to go out," she said, "and enjoy our private spring."

"It's cold," he said, "it's windy. The thing's too little—we'll never fit."

She looked exasperated, as if she'd discovered she'd married the world's most incorrigible panty-waist. "It's what we came for."

She opened the door and dashed naked into the winter gloaming. He pushed the door shut and disrobed. A moment later, when he lowered himself into the spring, he realized it was deeper than he'd imagined—it accommodated both of them easily. He wanted to tell her about the dying woman, her renewed attempt to reach the mountains, her husband's effort to redeem things. "Babe—" he said.

"Don't talk. I'm enjoying the heat."

He closed his eyes and leaned against the side of the pool. Steam invaded his nostrils. Jennifer shifted, so her long legs crossed his lap and rested there. When her hand encircled his member, he grasped her wrist, fearing his purchase on the world's sadness and his own deep implication in it might be contingent, that one sweaty embrace might steal that knowledge from him. "Jenn," he said, "I don't want this—"

"Shhhh," she said. "We came here for this, too."

She led him into the cabin, and they dried themselves, then reclined on the bed. While they shared a cigarette, he told her of the sick woman's pilgrimage. In the light from the stove, he saw tears gather at the corners of her eyes. "I'm going to light one of their candles," she said, striking a kitchen match. "And we'll make love in the light of it. I know it's bullshit, but I want to do it anyway."

"She's getting her last chance," she added, with a vehemence that made him reluctant again.

Seeing this, she kissed his neck, then worked downward. His reluctance disintegrated. Between her lips, his nipples enlivened, but it surprised him to feel the pinch of her incisors. She took him into her, and they moved together, and when they came she gnawed his small nubs fiercely. The pain alarmed him, but it conflated with his pleasure and made it keener. She hadn't done that before, and he wondered what sort of life force they'd beamed the unfortunate couple with *that* particular sex. "I wouldn't like it," she murmured, "if you did that to me." They napped until she roused him, desiring pleasure once more.

They ate dinner in Buena Vista, and when they returned, snow had started to fall, a sleety deluge that slapped their windshield. The driveway in front of Cabin Two was empty; the man and his dying wife hadn't arrived. Jennifer, drowsy from prime rib and beer, fell asleep as quickly as if she'd been hit by a tranquilizer dart. The candle had burned to a stub, so Mack ignited the second from its flame, then settled next to his wife, pulling her into an embrace. He could hear the river's purling, and her snoring mixed with that sound. His nipples still stung. He thought she'd hurt him to acknowledge whatever damage he'd caused was permanent, that his act, like hers, could not be undone. He couldn't prove that hypothesis, but it felt true. That she'd hurt him while giving pleasure made him believe she had forgiven him, in the partial way she'd forgiven herself.

But could *he* let go? Their second IVF had everything against it. But wasn't that the truth that made him most to blame? Five hundred chances in a thousand had resiliency. One chance in a thousand might be extinguished by an unkind look. As a scientist, he knew he'd question that idea. As a childless man, holding his childless lover, it seemed undeniable. And he was still learning of ways he'd failed.

He thought he heard tires crunching through snow, and he rose and slipped into his T-shirt and jeans, then stepped onto the porch, hoping the sick woman and her husband had come. But the adjoining cabin was dark. The wind had quit, and the snow had fattened to slow-falling flakes. Mack collected the candle and, shielding the flame, crossed the space between the cabins, the snow bitter against his feet. Through the window, he saw the couple's bed was undisturbed. Cabin Two was as empty as a diseased womb. In the glass, Mack could see his reflection. He thought of the hapless husband, losing his beloved. Imagined him, watching the Medivac climb. Meeting his boy's eyes, and believing that gaze would stay with him forever. Knowing details would have made the moment otherwise. Water, and oxygen.

He wondered whether the man could forgive himself. ✧

# Easter Weekend

Kenneth Cook

The family left for Aunt Velma's on Good Friday, shortly after lunch, because Mr. Tate got off work at noon. Mrs. Tate had already packed the suitcases and wrapped the ham she planned to cook for Easter dinner. Fay Wray—who'd been moping since their other dog Greta had run off— jumped around like an excited pup as they readied themselves for the trip, tongue lolling in a smile; she hopped in and out of the truck bed, barking. She was ready to go, right now, let's get on the road and head to Aunt Velma's and the farm, now, now, come on people, get moving.

Except for Laura's father, none of the family had been out of town since last Thanksgiving. Laura didn't realize how good it was to leave until they were on the highway, driving away—Mr. and Mrs. Tate with the three-year-old Rich up front, Laura and her brothers, Gene and Manny, and Fay in the back of the pickup with the luggage and the food, the sky white and breezy and cool, Charnelle dissolving behind them.

Aunt Velma wasn't really anybody's aunt. She was Mrs. Tate's second cousin by marriage. Uncle Unser, who was really Mrs. Tate's cousin, died in 1953. During World War II, where he'd served as a captain in the infantry, he lost the vision in his left eye and both his arms up to the elbows when a faulty grenade exploded in his hands as he withdrew the pin. He had metal hands attached at the VA and tried to return to normal life, but he couldn't do the farm work very efficiently nor, of course, the fiddle making, which he'd been famous for before he joined the military. He and Aunt Velma had never had children of their own, so they had always treated Laura's family like favorites. During the war, he'd sent them odd war remnants—pieces of shrapnel constructed into beautiful, strange collages, bullet casings with Italian and Russian lettering on the side, an Italian military sash for Laura's father. He even sent a German baby bracelet for Laura, who was born right before the end of the war. And even after he returned from the VA, he seemed extraordinarily good-natured, letting the kids touch his purple-striated stumps and even play with his metal hands as he sat on a stool or in his big leather chair, smiling serenely.

Mrs. Tate always referred to him as her uncle, as both a term of endearment and because he was almost twenty years older than she was. He'd always been, as she put it, a naturally happy man, quick with a joke or a tease.

So they were all shocked when Uncle Unser hanged himself in the barn. No note, no nothing. Aunt Velma found him swinging from the rafters one morning in May. Laura was sure there were explanations, but neither his death nor its possible causes were discussed with the kids. Manny told her that he thought Uncle Unser was an alcoholic; Laura said that was a big fat lie, and that he was just depressed, both from the war and from his inability to do what he most loved, and he didn't want to live anymore. It was that simple.

But it wasn't really so simple to Laura. She could never quite wrap her mind around that notion—not wanting to live—particularly since he seemed so obviously happy. There was some mysterious chasm between the man she had known and the man who had dangled from the rafters, like a secret self had taken over. It had bothered her for nearly a year— she even dreamed of it horribly, this demonic second self rising out of Uncle Unser's body and knotting the rope, loosening it over his neck— but then she had suddenly stopped thinking and dreaming about it altogether. As she grew older, it seemed more and more difficult to remember him very clearly, though every once in a while, especially when visiting Aunt Velma's, a charged memory would swim to the surface and overwhelm her for a few seconds—how his face looked like a sculpture, bronzed and creviced in the sunlight, or the sing-song way in which he sometimes spoke, or a snippet of one of his jokes, or his deadpan, teasing manner, his glass eye rolling loosely to one side while his good eye stared straight at you.


For supper, Aunt Velma and Mrs. Tate fixed catfish, okra, black-eyed peas, two pans of cornbread, and an apple cobbler for dessert. The kitchen smelled warm, buttery, sweet, and greasy. After Laura and Manny washed up, they all sat at the table, held hands, and Aunt Velma said an extended grace. Laura's family wasn't very religious, though they sometimes attended the Charnelle First Methodist Church. But Aunt Velma claimed that the Baptist church had saved her after Uncle Unser died, literally saved both her physical and spiritual lives, and she had devoted herself to volunteer work and to intensive study sessions with other members of the congregation, particularly those who'd lost spouses, parents, children, brothers, or sisters. Though Manny made fun of Aunt Velma's devotion, and her parents seemed to tolerate it respectfully, Laura was fascinated and often moved by Aunt Velma's fervor. Regardless of whether or not you believed what she believed, it was clear, to Laura at least, that it had changed Aunt Velma for the better—not like religion did for some people—made her generous and forgiving, and sustained her as she grew old, lit her from within rather than turning her cynical and ossified, as Laura, even as young as she was, could easily see happening to someone else in Aunt Velma's shoes. When your husband kills himself... well, no telling what could happen to you.

Aunt Velma reminded them that today, of all days, is what they must be grateful for, and she painted a vivid portrait of the frail Messiah, nearly naked, thorns digging into His skull, blood and sweat and dirt streaming into His eyes, which He could barely keep open, the spikes being driven through His hands and tender feet, and how the rabble of the town came to watch Him suffer, to throw stones and rotted vegetables, and as He faded into unconsciousness and death, the sky blackened. It was a day of torment and abject humiliation, but in this suffering were planted the seeds of the world's salvation.

"Amen," Mr. Tate said, and the kids, on cue, chimed in with their amens. Manny looked at Laura and rolled his eyes, smiling, and Laura smiled too, but felt bad about it, as if she was conspiring against Aunt Velma.

Saturday afternoon Mr. Tate took them all to see *The Ten Commandments,* a special event since they had never, as a family, been to an indoor movie theater before.

The Paladian Theater in Amarillo possessed its own special exoticism. It had just opened its doors, and Laura's father wanted to see a movie there because he had supervised a portion of the construction the previous fall. They arrived a good half hour before the film began, bought their tickets, and Mr. Tate spoke with the manager and then gave the family a tour of the theater, which seemed as thrillingly majestic as an English palace with its tall, red, crushed-velvet curtains, and the gold and black rococo curlicues on the facing of the balcony, and the curtain-covered screen, towering impressively above them, protected and veiled rather than exposed, like the drive-in screen, to the elements and insects and beer-swigging vandalism of adolescent boys.

Dressed sharply in a white shirt, jeans, and boots, Mr. Tate had spoken to and laughed with the manager like they were old friends, and then he strode about the empty theater like he owned it, pointing to the inlaid design of the balcony, explaining the joist work of the three pillars and steel-framed balcony support, which he himself had welded, rattling off the cost of the seats and the curtains and the screen, which indicated (Laura couldn't quite tell from her father's tone) either magnanimous wealth or a waste of money. At their father's insistence, Manny, Laura, and Gene clambered quickly up carpeted, spiral stairs to the balcony and leaned over the ledge, waving down to Rich, who stood smiling like a munchkin before the massive screen.

Before the show, they took their seats as other patrons filed in. Her father gave Manny and Laura three dollars and told them—in a clownish, mock-hick voice that made everybody laugh—to "oversee the movie vittles." They bought lemonade for their parents, Velma, and Rich, and A&W root beer for themselves and Gene, a brick of Hershey's chocolate for everybody to share, as well as two big bags of popcorn scooped from the reservoir of orange-yellow fluff.

The glass-covered light bulbs dimmed. The red curtain parted as the music from the first short, a Disney cartoon, trumpeted. Unlike the drive-in, the sound was not loud, but it was clear and staticless, the picture sharp without the crackles and lines and burn holes she had learned to ignore on the outdoor screen. The images brighter and more vivid, Laura thought, than real life.

A trailer for a black-and-white John Wayne western and then a newsreel, and then the movie itself. She hadn't quite known what to expect—a Technicolor sermon—but soon she was swallowed by the grand panoramic majesty of it all. It made her want to read the Bible. Who knew it was that romantic, that dramatic?

When they had arrived in early afternoon it had been hot and cloudless, but when they emerged from the theater over four hours later, the sun had slipped beneath the horizon. The sidewalk and grass glistened with rain, the sky milky purple, swollen and variegated as a two-day bruise. Laura felt disoriented. It was like falling asleep in the middle of the afternoon and awaking in the night, not sure what had happened or even what day it was. Time seemed to evaporate or be kidnapped. She didn't know if she liked this feeling—thick, narcotic, as palpable as an overripe melon.

Aunt Velma loved the movie, though she thought it a little racy for kids. Rich had fallen asleep. Manny loved the fights and the special effects, and Gene's favorite part was when Moses seemed to be walking around in a burning bush-induced glaze, his face red, his hair suddenly white. Mr. Tate thought it was way too long and had twice stepped outside to smoke a cigarette. Laura's mother liked the Exodus—the joy on all those people's faces when they finally left Egypt.

"What did you think, Laura?" Aunt Velma asked.

"I loved it."

"And your favorite part?"

"All of it," she said, but felt her answer disappointed everyone. They had given specifics, but she still felt too stunned by the experience to talk about it coherently.


Easter Sunday. They rose before dawn and went to the sunrise service at Aunt Velma's church, where the preacher recounted the old familiar story of the crucifixion, the days of darkness, the stone mysteriously moved from the cave, Jesus appearing to the women who loved Him and then later to His disciples, who needed testing, their hands in the holes of His body, and the final glorious ascension, hallelujah, hallelujah, amen.

Laura listened absently. She'd heard this story many times, and while on Friday, during Aunt Velma's dinner blessing, it had seemed fresh and alive, it now had lost its power to hold her attention. It seemed, in fact, pale and hackneyed compared to the movie they'd watched yesterday. She bent her head, as if in prayer, closed her eyes and tried to unfurl the movie in her mind. The most distinct images weren't the ones she would have thought: the Red Sea parting, Pharaoh's army stopped by the pillar of fire. She saw, instead, the more intimate moments—the princess playing that crazy game of Hounds and Jackals with the Pharaoh (it stunned her to think of Biblical figures playing board games); the gold dress "spun from the beards of shellfish"; Moses in chains in the dungeon, the princess prostrate before him; the dark shine of his sweaty body, half naked and caked in mud, in the immaculate throne room before his father, who turned away from him, who forbade the name of Moses to be mentioned again; Yul Brynner with that black snake of hair coiled exotically out of the side of his bald head.

Everyone suddenly stood and shuffled the hymnals in their hands. Laura opened her eyes and stood up, too, out of habit, and pretended to sing, "He arose, He arose, He arose," while a bright flicker of shame goosed over her because she'd been thinking about the movie, particularly Moses' sweat-glistened chest, instead of being thankful for Jesus dying to take away her sins.


After church, Mr. Tate took them fishing at the pond, but no one caught anything except Gene, who nabbed a little white perch. Aunt Velma, Mrs. Tate, and Laura made the dinner, and everyone played dominoes and canasta, ate watermelon that someone from church gave Aunt Velma, and then listened on the radio to an Easter special from the Grand Ole Opry in Nashville.

After cleaning the kitchen, Laura's mother wiped her hands and said, "I'm taking Fay for a walk."

Gene said, "I want to go." Both Laura and Manny looked on expectantly, like they, too, could use a walk before the trip home.

"No, you stay here," she said and was out the screen door before anyone could answer.

"Aw, come on," Gene said, moving toward the door.

Aunt Velma caught his arm. "You come sit with me, honey."

"But I want to go."

"Come sit here in this chair with me. Let your mother have a little time to herself."


At almost eight, their mother still hadn't returned. Mr. Tate, Manny, and Gene were loading the truck for the return trip. Laura helped Aunt

Velma dry the last of the dishes and wrap the leftovers they were going to take back to Charnelle.

Laura's father came in and asked, "Where's your mother?"

"I don't know."

"Well, go find her and tell her it's time to go."

Laura dried her hands, put on her sweater, and walked across the dark meadow, calling for her mother and Fay. She walked to the orchard where the light from the barn crept to the edge of the trees, but she didn't go into the grove, not at night. She heard rustling off in the branched shadows. She called again. A flurry of indistinct movement, then some animal, a coyote maybe, scrambled out of the panoply of trees. Laura sucked in her breath and backpedaled quickly, thinking the animal was charging toward her. But when Laura glanced again, she saw it lope in the opposite direction, as afraid as she was, moonlight skittering across the edge of its neck and head. It disappeared over a hill.

She felt apprehensive, jumpy, so she walked swiftly, calling again. The evening had cooled; her breath misted in front of her. A twig snapped, and she broke into a run toward the faint light of the barn, where the chickens chastised her when she entered. Genevieve, the Holstein, mooed loudly, and Laura, in the midst of this animal chorus, felt suddenly ridiculous. She laughed nervously and then heard the familiar wheezing bark of Fay, and said, "Fay? Momma?"

The gloomy one-bulb light of the barn was creepy. From the hay-strewn corner, Fay emerged surprisingly, as if passing through a watery membrane separating darkness from light, and walked up to Laura and licked her hand. She bent down and rubbed the dog's chin, and Fay immediately lay down on her back and exposed her belly for more scratching.

"Where's Momma?" she asked the dog, who closed her eyes and lifted her paws. Laura peered into the darkness and could vaguely make out a still, human shape, and a quick shuddering dread whipped through her.

"Momma, is that you?"

"Yes."

Laura walked toward her and could see her mother sitting against a bale of hay. Why hadn't she answered her calls or said anything? Laura wondered how long her mother had been here. Had she watched Laura running into the barn? It frightened her, this strange silence. In the shadows, her mother's cheeks shimmered, shiny and wet.

"Are you okay?" Laura asked.

She didn't answer.

"Momma, are you okay?"

"Yes, Laura."

"Why are you crying?"

She wiped her face with her sleeve and said, "I'm not."

"What is it?"

Her mother rose and walked into the light. "I didn't realize it'd gotten so late. Is it time to go?"

"Oh, my God," Laura shouted. "You're bleeding!"

Her mother's yellow blouse was ripped below her left ribs. A blot of darkened blood encircled the ragged hole. Laura reached out and touched the stain.

Her mother pulled her back sharply. "Don't do that."

"What happened?" she asked. The blood felt warm and greasy on her fingers.

"I caught it on some barbed wire. Dumb. It's nothing. We better get going. Come on, Fay."

The dog stood sleepily, hay clinging to her back, and fell in step at Mrs. Tate's heels.

"You, too, Laura."

"But Momma—"

Her mother, however, was already through the barn gate, striding across the meadow toward the distant, phosphorescent light of the house. Laura followed, but her mother moved fast, dissolving into the darkness until both she and the dog seemed merely gold-lined silhouettes.


On the drive home, Laura, Manny, and Gene wore their wool caps and mufflers and huddled together with Fay under the two afghans Aunt Velma had given them. Gene fell asleep, and she and Manny watched the shifting stars as the truck hummed north along the highway back to Charnelle. With the wind and the sound of the truck's tires on the asphalt, it was too loud for talk, which suited Laura just fine because she liked this time without words. Lying flat in the bed, they could see the headlights from passing cars and trucks shining over them like spotlights. The sky had cleared, and she took a delight in identifying the constellations she knew and searching for new ones, which she gave foolish names she soon forgot.

She could tell they were close to Charnelle at least ten minutes before they arrived. The traffic going the other way increased, and the sky brightened from the lights. She sat up and peered through the cab window. The tip of her father's cigarette glowed orange and brightened when he inhaled. Rich was asleep in their mother's lap, and Mrs. Tate had her head turned toward the side window to the low dark hills that rose and toppled as they sped along. Laura rubbed her fingers together. Though she couldn't see them, she knew they were still stained with her mother's blood. In the scramble to get going, she had forgotten to wash it off. She put them to her nose but smelled nothing.

What was her mother thinking about? Laura wondered. She wished she could get inside her mother's head for just a few minutes and see what was going on in there, but that was impossible, she knew, just as she understood that others would never be able to see into her thoughts and that, even if they asked her outright, she would never be able to express them in a way they could fully understand.

Through both the cab window and the front window, she could see the lights of Charnelle spread across the plains like a long prairie fire, flickering and blinking and calling them home. Tomorrow she'd be back in school, back to the familiar routines of classes and chores and the chattery, joking banter with her friends at lunch. That would be fine and good, she knew, but she wasn't there yet, and the weekend itself, the reason they had gone, the fun they'd had, was over, and there was only this between time of traveling in the dark.

A wave of sadness swept through her. She didn't know if it was the weekend ending, or worries about her mother, or tiredness, perhaps, and she was prone to these quick spells of sadness or confusion. She often felt a strange, conflicting pull to either give into the spells—"wallow in it," as her father said—or to resist it, shake it off, get up and do something, anything, which did seem to work: motion triumphing over mood.

Gene and Manny, asleep on either side of her now, turned at the same moment and tugged the afghans from her, sending a whistling chill through her bones. She pulled the covers back, nestling against Fay's warm fur. She absently stroked the dog as she watched the sky lighten from behind, the town seeming to curl over the cab into the truck bed.

After pulling into the gravel driveway, Mr. Tate turned off the truck, which rattled and shook Gene and Manny awake. The silence after the drive seemed suddenly cottony and thick. Her father said something to her, but she couldn't understand and had to yawn several times to unplug her ears.

Gene wobbled sleepily, and Laura helped him to bed. Her father put Rich in his crib, and after helping unload everything into the living room, Laura slipped into her nightgown and, falling asleep, the sadness from before was replaced now by a grateful warmth, the familiar pleasure of the journey finally ended, of returning home, of being home. The cool, sculpted contours of her mattress held her like a soft hand and urged her to sleep. ✧

# Sugar

Nelly Reifler

"What's in the box?" Mother asked. She was standing by the closet door. She held the door open with her hip. I looked down at her brown shoes with their spongy soles. I had not heard her come up the carpeted stairs. I had been caught. "It's her, isn't it," Mother said, "it's Sugar." She poked at the box with her foot. It was in the closet, on the bottom shelf, next to a pile of folded sweaters.

"She'll wake up," I whispered. Actually, she was already awake. I looked at my own feet, dangling under where I sat on my bed. I looked at the shiny black Mary Janes and white cuffed socks against the pale pink chenille of the bed spread. My shoes had hard soles, heels with taps on them. I could not come and go silently.

"Stay right there," said Mother. She backed out of the room, keeping her eyes on me. She yelled down to Daddy, "Frederick, we need you up here."

I knew what would happen next. I dropped off the bed and dashed for the closet. *Sugar's box!*—I picked it up and hugged it. She was starting to move in the box. She had been asleep for days, and time had passed quietly in the house. Now I could feel her stretching her limbs, could feel her nails scratching against the cardboard as she stretched. There was also the low noise of bristly fur brushing against itself. I could feel where her head pressed against the end of the box, and I heard the exhalation of a Sugar yawn. I felt my heart beat against my chest. I didn't want them to take her away again.

Mother reappeared in the room. "I told you not to move," she said. I pressed my face against the side of the box. I backed into the closet. I felt Sugar's alertness inside the box. She was not moving much, but she was listening. I sat down in the corner, between the hems of my winter coat and my long dress. The closet smelled like camphor and cedar. Daddy appeared behind Mother at the closet door. Inside the closet, it was very dark, and the rest of the room was filled with white sunlight: Daddy and Mother were just silhouettes.

Daddy leaned towards the closet. "How's my girl," he said, "my pumpkin? Kitten? Sweet Pea?" I said nothing. "How's my angel? My valentine?" I whispered, "Fine." Sugar shifted inside the box.

"Why don't you just come out like a good girl and give Daddy the box," he said. Sugar shifted again.

"She's not going to do it, Frederick," said Mother. "You know how it is."

Sugar knocked against the inside of the box with her head. I squeezed the box tight. A tiny fist punched the wall of the box.

Sugar was fine in my closet.


Every day, I woke up with Mother's eyes on me. She had my school clothes waiting for me. I had seven dresses, one for each day of the week. Plus my long party dress, for the one day each year that Mother and Daddy called my birthday. On this day, they told me I was a year older, and I blew out candles on a cake. The number of candles was always different. One year there might be thirteen candles, and the next, there would be seven.

After I dressed and ate my toast each morning, I would cross the cul-de-sac to go to school. I always turned my head and stared down the long road, a perfectly straight ribbon of pavement with no other houses on it. A deep forest was on the other side of this road, next to the schoolhouse. Something about the density of the trees, whose roots pressed against the low stone wall, always made me linger before Daddy or Mother tugged at my hand and pulled me into the schoolhouse.

Daddy would complain about the expense of educating me, but they agreed it was important to have me properly schooled. Three walls of the schoolhouse were lined with book shelves, divided into different subjects: Math, Science, Vocabulary, Penmanship. On the back wall there was a blackboard. Every day, detailed instructions were left for me in perfect script letters in white chalk on this board. They told which books to take from the shelves, which chapters to read, which words to study. Daddy and Mother would take turns checking in to make sure I was doing the lessons.

Sometimes the vocabulary or math books hinted at something. Words that I could not reconcile stayed with me: *post office, bus, puppy, roller-skate, freight train, teacher.* I would consider these words and day-dream, staring at the dust between the threads of a binding, or looking out the window at the forest behind the school house. But my work was checked each night, after supper. I could not drift off very long.

While they discussed my notes downstairs, I would go and visit with Sugar in the closet, waking her by whispering her name until she came to silent attention in her box. We would stay like this for three quarters of an hour, listening to each other's wakefulness and breath.

They had taken her away once, but she came back. In the short time since she had returned, she awakened easily, was noisier and stronger. Daddy and Mother would enter and leave the room silently, inspecting and observing. But now, whenever they approached me, she woke up and listened. Whenever they spoke to me in a certain way, I could feel her moving in the box, alert.

I was not supposed to have her in the first place. She came late at night after a strange evening at the house. It was after dinner, and Daddy and Mother had been checking my notes. I sat at my desk, looking out the window at the endless lawn behind the house. It was an expanse of even green, nothing to see besides grass, no buildings or trees in the distance. I heard voices rise downstairs. Mother and Daddy were arguing. I had never heard them argue. I crept out of my room and stood silently on the landing, and for once, they couldn't hear me over their own noise. They were standing at the dining table. At first, I could only see Mother, but then Daddy's hand appeared and grabbed her wrist. I ran downstairs and into the dining room. I took my mother's other wrist and pulled, trying to get her away from him. She laughed an unfamiliar laugh, and shook herself free of Daddy easily. She turned towards me without really looking at me. Then she picked me up and carried me upstairs. It was impossible to move in her arms. She took me to my desk, put me down in the chair forcefully, squeezed my fingers around a pencil, and left the room.

I sat there. My heart was pounding. I made a tight fist around the pencil, then let go. The pencil dropped, and I watched the blood rush back into my palm.

Later that night, as I lay in bed, thoughts entered my head like transmitted radio signals. I tried not to listen to them, but there they were, speaking, whispering: You are you, you are you, not them, but you. There is more, there is more, there is more than this. You are you, you are you . . . .

I woke up in the middle of the night to the sound of scratching. I had forgotten what happened earlier and the thoughts that had repeated in my head. I opened my eyes and saw the bluish, moonlit box on my window sill. The sound was coming from inside it.

Now Daddy stepped from behind Mother and put his head into the closet. "It's time, Pumpkin," he said. He chucked me under the chin; Sugar banged with a fist inside the box. Daddy tried to chuckle. He slowly reached over to ruffle my hair—then—Bang. Bang. Bang. He jumped back from the closet, and stood behind Mother.

"Listen," Mother said, "Isn't it easier to hand the box over than to have it taken away?" Sugar paused, listening. I shook my head and clutched the box. "We don't want to have to do this," said Mother.

Daddy said, "Let's just wait for her to go to sleep again."

"No, Frederick, she's expecting us now. She'll never move from that closet."

They both backed to the corner of the room. They whispered to each other, all the while keeping their eyes on me. Sugar was scraping her nails against the cardboard. Slow, sharpening sounds. I pressed my lips against the bulge in the cardboard where her head was, and its roundness made me feel safe. Mother and Daddy approached the closet again. Their steps were measured. Sugar's scratching paused. We waited. Mother lunged for my arms, and Daddy reached for the box, his cuffs rolled down to protect his hands—Bang. Bang. Bang. Bang. Sugar punched and kicked. Daddy dropped the box back into my lap. The punching and kicking got faster. Mother let go of me and tried to pick up the box herself, but it was vibrating too much in her arms. She dropped the box. They moved away from the closet once more and returned to the doorway. Sugar's banging slowed and stopped. We listened to silence.

Mother's voice was different when she spoke again. Low. Soft. Even-toned. "You're going to do a relaxation exercise," she said to me. Sugar and I listened. We had never heard Mother's voice like this before. "I want you to close your eyes," she said, "and imagine you're somewhere very safe."

I tried not to close my eyes, but I found I could not keep them open.

"Imagine you're somewhere very safe," she said again. I imagined I was inside my closet, holding Sugar's box. I imagined she was inside the box, awake but silent, protecting me. "Now," Mother said, "imagine you're in this safe place, and your limbs are getting very heavy. Say to yourself, 'I am going to relax my toes. My toes are relaxing. My toes are relaxed.'"

I imagined myself standing up and walking past Mother and Daddy, who were frozen like statues, not dead, but still.

"I'm going to relax my knees. My knees are relaxing. My knees are relaxed."

I imagined myself walking down the stairs, barefoot, making no noise. I imagined myself going to the front door. It was unlocked, and I opened it easily. I stood at the door for a moment, then I stepped onto the lawn. The grass was soft under the soles of my feet.

*I'm going to relax my hips. My hips are relaxing. My hips are relaxed.* I imagined that I walked across the lawn and got to the edge of the paved road, where I looked down at a gutter clogged with leaves. Then I walked across the cul-de-sac. The rough pavement was hot from the sun.

*I am going to relax my shoulders. My shoulders are relaxing. My shoulders are relaxed.* The door to the schoolhouse was open, but I walked around the building to the forest.

*I am going to relax my neck. My neck is relaxing. My neck is relaxed.* There was a low stone wall at the edge of the forest. I stepped up onto it, still carrying Sugar's box. Cool air came from the trees, and there was a damp, growing mushroom smell. The other side of the stone wall dropped further, so I had to climb down backwards. Then I turned and walked into the forest. The ground was covered with pine needles. There was a slope to the forest floor, and as I descended, the cul-de-sac disappeared behind me. Soon I found myself next to a brook. I sat on a rock and watched the streaming water split smoothly around twigs and stones. I thought, 'This would be a good place to let Sugar go,' and I took her box over to a safe circle of reeds growing near the water. I set the box down and walked away from it along the bank. All along the water, red flowers grew and clustered, four or five long stems together, with a spike of color on the end of each stem. The flowers were closed, petals pressing against each other like pods.

*I'm going to relax my hands. My hands are relaxing. My hands are relaxed.* I vaguely felt a tugging, heard familiar voices gurgling under the water. "I've got it," one of them said. Another said, "Well take it away. And dig a deep enough hole this time."

I considered the flowers, and a word came to me. Snapdragon. Snapdragons. I had seen a picture of them once in a book at school. I bent down and touched a pod of petals. It was firm on the outside, and the petals were closed tight. I squeezed it between two fingers. It snapped open and showed a tender red center. I put a finger in the flower. It was soft now, slightly downy.

I was alone. It was all right. Sugar would come back to me. If she didn't, I would go and find her. ✧

# Bargain Donuts

Chloe Bland

In lieu of a conventional exercise regime, and as a course of dodging another summer spent tallying groceries with the Brainy Bunch—as he called the retarded baggers—opposite aisle eight, behind which his wife, the meat cutter, cut meat, he crossed the country in search of the best donut bargains, which is how he got calves the Boise bakery girls took note of when they bent down for refresher rolls of register tape.

He walked in a pair of ten-year-old sneakers and only accepted rides from truckers because they had crude humor and beds inside the cabs.

In Connecticut, he bought three supermarket crullers for $1.90, but they were small and stale. Not like the cinnamon rolls he found at a truck stop in Ohio—two big catcher's mitts for $1.99. Well worth the additional nine cents, he wrote his father on a post card of the Delaware River Water Gap.

Peoria was pricey—three thick cakey jelly sticks were going for $3.89 at a bakery with cats sleeping in the window, but that included a cup of coffee. He was largely disappointed by Iowa and Kansas and in Colorado, at least for a long stretch through the mountains, altitude sickness made him forgo donuts altogether. In El Paso, he'd filled up on McDonald's apple pies. They tasted of nutmeg and nostalgia, like the air in Idaho, where he'd grown up for one year when he was seven.

But none of this could compare to the donuts he would discover in San Francisco. For $2.99 he purchased five glazed donuts, still warm, that surpassed any form of fried dough he'd ever tasted, including the spiced, deep-fried button mushrooms he ate a bucket of at his own wedding.

After licking his fingers he sat on a bench and wrote to his wife, who would undoubtedly be dying to know if he had gotten the donut deals out of his system and when he would be coming home. He signed off, Love, Gerry, and thought of the Brainy Bunch, who would feel sad not to get their T-shirts (all six from different cities)—sadder, even, than his wife not to get him, now that he was onto something—and he thought of how they called him: Joy. ✧

# NONFICTION

POST ROAD

# Apology to Henry Aaron

Steven Church

Henry Aaron, when you smacked homerun number 715 into the lights, fans dropped to the evergreen field and ran after you. I know you've seen the film footage that I've seen, pictures that promised a moment of pure joy. The roar of the crowd. The drop of jaws. The drop of drinks and hot dogs. This one white fan—his wild hair flying and toothy smile. The first one there. He jumps from his seat. Legs pumping, he gallops for the infield. You trot around the bases, waving to the crowd. You've just knocked the Babe from his throne. You don't even see him coming. And he's just this loose-limbed image of happiness—or at least that's what I thought, that's what I believed.

He must have seen the homerun before it even left your bat, right in mid-swing. The swipe of the stick, the path of the ball—and he knew Ruth's record was gone. I imagine he'd been following your record march, chalking up dingers on his wall at home, maybe scratching them into the back of his bedroom door. He could be nineteen years old, still living in his widowed mother's basement. For a ticket to the game, maybe he traded his most prized possession—a miniature bicycle built for him by his Chinese neighbor. Maybe he loved this bicycle with its tiny rubber-band tires, spokes made from copper wire, and a frame bent from a clothes hanger. Maybe this man and his neighbor watched you Saturdays on television. He taught her words like strike, ball, bullpen, fastball, slider. She taught him the secret of silence, the trick to dancing with houseflies. His mother paid her for piano lessons. But the teacher sat beside him on the bench while he practiced. Her hand on his leg, her finger reading the inseam of his jeans, she whispered the play-by-play from your baseball games. She whispered words she had memorized from game-day recordings he slipped into her mailbox after dark. Aaron steps up to the plate. The two-two pitch. He swings. And, oh baby, it's outta here. She made miniature toys she could have sold to emperors. She built a tiny bicycle for two. She told stories with her hands.

But now . . . she would never forgive this foolish man who skipped his lesson, left her arms, pushed his way up to the wall, and waited for the hard crack of ball to bat. What about the bicycle between them? There's nothing musical about his leaving. But for him it was always about you, Henry Aaron. He would have given anything for this moment, even a bicycle token. Maybe like me as a child, this white boy dreamed only of black heroes. Maybe he, too, read only biographies of black athletes. His mother probably didn't understand why it was so important. She never knew a thing of Babe Ruth, the white giant. She sat at home, reluctantly tuning her radio to the game. And maybe all of this would make a difference if it were true.

Whatever the reason, whatever he left behind, this man was there to see your swing, Henry. He had a jump on the ball and ran hard to catch you between second and third base. You just trotted around the diamond, waving to the crowd, not gloating about it. That wasn't your way. And then he burst into the picture and slapped you hard on the shoulder. You turned at the last second. And I like to imagine that he called you "Mr. Aaron." I wish he'd said something beautiful—something to fit the image given me by the television cameras. I don't know what he was thinking. But I do know now what you thought. I've heard your words recently, Mr. Aaron.

What should have been your proudest moment had already been soiled by repeated phone calls to your home, threats whispered into the receiver. And I believed that this young man, stupid with joy, his limbs all loose in the rush of pride, just wanted to share your triumph—as if he was saying for all of us, you are the greatest. But you, Henry Aaron—just for a split second—you believed that he had come to kill you, put a bullet in your head right there on the field in front of teammates and the world. I heard your words some twenty years later, saw this moment through different eyes. I realized again the false promises of television. And I apologize for this fan—for his grin, his gait, his slap. I apologize for his dreams, his color, and my belief. I apologize to his imaginary Chinese lover. I apologize because it sounds like lies. I apologize for writing. But there's something about your memory I just can't shake. ✧

# A Letter to the Bionic Man

Steven Church

Steve Austin, who stitched your orange jumpsuit with patches? As a boy I wanted some, too—those embroidered badges of courage and health. I wanted to hear the whisper of doctors: *We can rebuild him. We have the technology.* Dad used to say my knees were baseballs bulging out. And I've seen you powder a baseball with your fist, crush it down to dust until the leather sloughs off like blistered skin. I bet you could've done the same to me.

I've witnessed your recovery from a rolling, flaming wreck—your airplane ripped up on the tarmac and that muffled TV voice, *he's breaking up, he's breaking up.* They plumbed your astronaut limbs with steel, wired your veins, gave you circuits for nerves. *We can make him better, stronger, faster.* I needed robotic bones, too. In Mrs. Ricket's class, a virus grabbed my legs, shot pain through my shins. I crumpled in front of the classroom sink. My face broke out with fever blisters, my sinuses clogged with infection. Doctor Pete gave me antibiotics, but I was confused because I thought he gave me *antibionics* and I knew I didn't want these. But you, Steve Austin, you never suffered from fever dreams like me. You never boiled at one-hundred-and-five, went limp in your mother's arms. You leap over chain link fences and oncoming traffic. You pulse with a beeping sound—like the electronic drum of a heart. Your bionic eye never misses danger on the horizon.

Steve Austin, I know you make love to a bionic woman who owns a bionic German Shepherd. I've seen the two of you together in the park. She crushes tennis balls with her fist, jumps fences, and pulses just for you. With her one robotic ear, she hears clearly the whispered plots of criminals, the stealthy approach of enemies, oncoming trains—all with bionic drum and cochlea. Maybe the two of you live together in a bionic suburbia. And at night, when robotic Bigfoot has returned to the hills, when the prime-time criminals are sleeping, the two of you sit by a fire oiling your parts. Maybe you talk about the curse of super-senses, the problem with bionic R.E.M. Can your parts keep up with your brain? Can they pulse fast enough? I imagine you must wear an eyepatch to sleep—the thin skin of your eyelid nearly transparent to your robotic pupil. And I'm sorry for your insomnia. I'm sorry for the pain of bone screws.

But at least your bionic mate is there by your side, stitching patches to your suit. She shares your pain and discomfort. She, too, must compensate for technology. Maybe she packs her ear with foam at night, or switches it off somehow. I hate to think what she hears—neighbors brushing their teeth, the dilation of your bionic eye, the spawn of mosquitoes in the creek out back. They pop like corn in the night. And maybe she hears me, too, with my baseball knees, my sickened head full of fevers. Because I am still there on the swing-set you built for show. I pump my hips on the rocker-swing until the squeaking brings you to the window. The two of you stand there—you with your eyepatch and she with her ear full of cotton. You might wrap your arm around her shoulder, kiss her wet cheek. You might whisper soft words in her normal ear— because I look very much like the bionic baby you'll never have. ✧

# A River in Charleston

Ashley Shelby

**B**arbara slim and smiling. Donald goofy and even slimmer. Barbara's thick black hair, beautifully parted. Her eyes, round like river stones, shining under lids of blue eye shadow. Donald happy to be there, be-suited and clear-eyed. They posed for a snapshot under an orange and green plastic lampshade, their new wedding bands shining in the light. It was a December night in 1974, and the couple stood in the kitchen of their beach cottage on Sullivan's Island, across the Cooper River from Charleston, South Carolina.

One spring, I had a dream about Charleston. It was a kaleidoscopic blend of gardens and hanging moss, of Southern estates and an old wedding photograph. I remember something soft from that dream, a gentle push to the road and the presentation of a hologram of my parents, which I was to investigate. And, with Sean on the road with me, I felt up to a trip to this fiercely Southern, DAR-lovin' confederate outpost.

We pack my old Tempo, and I take the wheel. We follow the river from Indiana into Ohio, where Highway 52 clings close to the Ohio River. Boys are playing a game of football in a field that lay next to the river, and I see a touch football star emerging in a spirited touchdown sprint...a touch football star in a snowy Cincinnati field on the Ohio River.

Donald was a boy in Indiana, but he was a plutonic post-adolescent just north of this snowy riverbank. Sandwiched between Clifton Avenue and Jefferson Avenue in the heart of Cincinnati, Donald spent three and a half years in college. He dated a ballerina who pierced his ear with a sewing needle, an ice cube, and the promise of sex afterwards. His right ear was bloodied, but the ballerina was too tired to keep her promise that night. Years later, to amuse his daughters, Donald would stick fishing lures through the hole in his ear.

Sean and I exit through the belly of Ohio into West Virginia. Toward mid-afternoon, we enter hill country and pass through villages as flimsy as afterthoughts, barely more than façades. The slopes of backyards are graveyards of debris. A pink mattress covered in mud and a pink box spring with a gaping tear in its side, split milk crates, children's toys, tires, all sliding into the stream that bubbles by the road where they've set up plank footbridges or ladders. The neighborhoods are villages, wedged into a topographic crease, a forgotten wrinkle in the Allegheny Mountains. We continue east to Charleston, to twin rivers, towards a wedding photograph.

Barbara and Donald slept together before they were married. They kept it a secret from Barbara's mother, who would never have approved. Barbara and Donald lived in a tiny white beach house on Sullivan's Island just across the Cooper River from Charleston, South Carolina. Don was an alcoholic. Barbara was pretty. They lived in sin and ate crab every night because they couldn't afford anything else.

It is close to midnight as I wind my way through a North Carolina thicket. There is something strange about night travel. When the journey continues as the day ends, you feel you're traveling on the underbelly of time; it's a darker, more enigmatic side of the journey. And in that moment before everything is black, and you see only the outline of life you're leaving behind for a few days, or forever, a shadow appears and follows you until the memory of what's behind leaves in favor of the anticipations of what's to come. I've never been good at leaving memories behind. Instead, I seek out the memories of others. It keeps me on that underbelly of time.

Donald was angular and skinny with early morning, skylight eyes. He had a moustache when he lived in Charleston. He shaved it off when his first child was born a few years later. Donald drank a lot. He treated Barbara like a queen, and she didn't think it was odd that he finished off a six-pack every night. She also did not think it odd that he would stop by the house at noon, have a few beers, and then go back to work. That was just the way it was. Men drank back then, Barbara said. Everyone did.

Pink has turned into indigo night when I pull the Tempo onto narrow George Street in Charleston and into the driveway of the inn where the manager is just locking up. He waves us over and hands me a key. I take it and walk into our hotel room with my bag and Barbara's map to Sullivan's Island.

Sean takes a shower, and I hear him gasp when the water suddenly becomes ice cold, then grows so hot it scalds him. I laugh for the first time that day. He comes out of the bathroom with a pink towel wrapped round his waist. His body is shiny and wet, and he smells like good soap. His lips are always cold and wet when he steps out of the shower and he always has a cold, wet kiss for me then. I stare at his body, which is straight as a ruler, surrendering not to a curve or indentation at the hip or waist. Before we left for Charleston I made him cheese grits, scrambled eggs, and fed him pizza and french fries, but he seemed only to grow thinner.

Barbara used to make big dinners for Donald, who was over six feet tall and weighed just 135 pounds. He was spindly too, but an excellent athlete—an Indiana high school basketball star and a champion butterflier and backstroke wizard. Donald also played quarterback on his high school football team and was a sectional finalist in the pole vault, which he took up that very year. But he was skinny, and no amount of beer would change that.

I pull the heavy wooden shutters off the windows that open onto George Street. It's warm outside and the scent of lilac and magnolia blossoms floats into the room. We walk down George Street and turn onto Meeting Street—narrow and lined with short, old-town storefronts that have become Gaps and Saks Fifth Avenues. But we don't mind because we're happy to be warm and clean and seeing palm trees dipping and bowing in the breeze. We stroll past an old cemetery. The walls are high, but the odd brick has fallen out, and I peer through into the graveyard garden. Spanish moss hangs from tree branches, grazing the tops of elaborate headstones.

Donald was drunk in ten minutes that first time. He was only fourteen but chose to take on Seagram's VO whiskey. He drank about three-quarters of the bottle. He was at a pool party. They had a liquor cabinet on wheels and it was pushed against the wall and he pulled it out and pretended like he was drinking with the capped bottle. *Go ahead go ahead do it do it.* Everyone egged him on, daring him, so he did it because he wanted them to like him. So he did and he got sick—but before he got sick something happened. The alcohol made him feel better than he ever had in his whole life. With three-quarters of a bottle of whiskey in him, he didn't have to be Donald. He didn't care what his parents thought, what his coaches thought—he didn't care what any of them saw when they looked at him. The disappointment written on their faces, the failures they brought to his attention, the accusations of arrogance—all of it, erased.

When he sobered up, he was sick, but he was also Donald again. He hadn't realized how much he didn't want to be Donald. Not until he had that time when he wasn't.

We've got to get to Sullivan's Island, I tell Sean the next morning, carefully unfolding Barbara's map, which has suffered a tear at the corner from having been folded and refolded too many times. I tell Sean I want to take a nice black and white photograph of the house. He asks me why it's so important, and I tell him that my parents lived here when they were just a few years older than us and ate crab and lived in sin. Sean asks me if we're living in sin. I'm not sure. Sin is relative to the times, I offer. But I'm uncertain, and in Barbara's skin again if not simply borrowing her eyes round like river stones and her taste for skinny, kind men. Sean and I decide to venture over the Cooper River to Sullivan's Island the next day.

Donald didn't want to be Donald. In high school, his friends thought it was cool that he could throw back so many beers, but no one in his family knew. They didn't pay much attention to Donald because he was the youngest. Something happens when you're the youngest, Donald used to say. Parents pay very close attention to their first child. They have high expectations and are extremely attentive. The second child is generally independent and free. When Donald appeared unexpectedly, born ten years after his brother Bob and twelve years after his sister Sally, his parents had already been through the messes of children and were not as interested in him as they had been in their other children. He was a mistake. *The mistake.* They said: here's Bob, here's Sally. And here is Donald, the mistake. Everybody would laugh. Donald laughed, too. It was their attention that he needed. He wanted them to approve of him, to respect him, to admire him. But it was hard to get their attention. Dad was either working or reading. Mom was at her bridge club. Maybe that's why he started to drink. He'd have to think about it.

That evening Sean and I sit in the wharf of the Ashley River. I tell Sean that I was named after the river that is passing in the moonlight before us—Ashley. My sister Lacy was expected to be a boy, and her name was to be Cooper, after the Cooper River. My youngest sister, Delta, was named after the triangular spot of silt found at the mouth of rivers. I thought it very romantic when Donald told me of the allusions we'd carry in our names forever. But Barbara told me that for Delta, at least, her name was less about a river and more about a song by Helen Reddy called

"Delta Dawn." I was named after this river, though, and sometimes at night, when I cling to my dreams of water, I swim in my name.

Barbara left her government job in Washington, packed up her car, put her hyperactive Irish Setter in the back seat and followed Donald to Charleston. She found a job with the Charleston branch of the Defense Department and settled into a routine. Yes, she did get concerned from time to time when Donald would get terribly drunk and act like a fool. He was an embarrassment. Many times Barbara would leave a party without him. They had their ups and downs with booze; they'd fight about it, he'd apologize, she'd forgive him and want to believe that it was okay. Sometimes Donald told Barbara that he didn't believe he'd live long. *I don't think I'll live a day past thirty-two*, he'd tell her. Thirty-two was still six years away, though. There was time to change, but there was also time to kill.

Sean and I walk past the old graveyard, and I sneak into the courtyard of its round church. The gate is open and a cat is lounging on a stone step; it is an open invitation. The headstones are crumbling and the inscriptions thick with moss. One usually ponders mortality and the fragility of life when in a graveyard, but there is something about a Southern cemetery that wipes the philosopher right out of you.

The next morning, before the sun is above the palmettos on King Street, Sean and I leave our inn in the Tempo, which has the dust of six states on its wheels. I unfold Barbara's map and study it. The lines are drawn in wobbly, haphazard trajectories toward the edges of the paper. I see a squiggle, which represents the Cooper River, and two blunt lines across the squiggle that are the Cooper River bridges—first Pearlman Memorial Bridge, then the Ben Sawyer Bridge. I dislodge a new, plastic-covered map of "Charleston and surrounding areas" from between my seat and the shift and study the streets of Sullivan's Island. *Poe Avenue. Raven Drive. Goldbug Avenue.*

Donald's favorite bar was called The Gold Bug, just up the road from Raven Drive and Poe Avenue. He spent many nights there with buddies from work, but Barbara never stepped foot inside. When she got home from work in the evening, she'd set the table and make dinner for two. In the beginning, Donald would come home after work and eat with her. It was nice. But then he started missing dinner a few times a week. Barbara kept setting his place at the table and kept making dinner for two. Donald missed more and more dinners, and one night, Barbara stopped setting a place for him. She knew where he was, and had been, those nights when he didn't come home. Sometimes Donald would call Barbara from The Gold Bug and blather senselessly and she'd scream at him, asking him if he had any idea how long she'd been waiting for him. But she never went up the street to drag him home. She didn't want to make a scene. He'd be home eventually.

And then there were the parties where Donald burned brightly and dazzled everyone with the charisma that he used like an amulet, a charm that grew tarnished the more he drank. Barbara, though comfortable in Donald's shadow, might step toward him late in the evening, put a gentle hand on his shoulder and whisper that he'd had too much to drink. I didn't know it was your job to count, he'd say, and she'd shrink back into the shadow. When she was away from the parties and Donald's drinking, she read and reread *The Great Gatsby* and, fancying herself Zelda Fitzgerald, took to smoking her menthols in a cigarette holder.

Sean and I reach the river in a flash, and as we drive over the Pearlman Bridge, the Cooper glints in my eyes. The reed beds are already thick, and the pungent smell of riverbed fills my nostrils. We touch land for only a moment, and then we are on the Ben Sawyer Bridge. I look back at the map and see Barbara has drawn a lopsided box on the left side of the Ben Sawyer highway. She marked it as WCIV-TV. Slow down here, I say to Sean. Better pull into the parking lot. We do and stare open-mouthed at the tiny brick box marked WCIV-TV. I tell Sean that Donald started his television career here.

Six years after Donald left this television station, after he'd been through the Houston television market, moved to Minnesota's top-twenty market, and fathered three girls with river names, he got drunk on television. March 28th, 1980. He was doing the weekend shows and in between the six and ten p.m. reports one night, he went out and got drunk at the bar across the street from the station. He came back, went on the air, and couldn't read the script. His producers were scared for their jobs and brought him into the general manager's office. The general manager told Donald that he could go to treatment and the station would pay for it and he could come back to work when he got sober. Or, if Donald didn't get treatment, he'd fire him that night and spend the rest of his life seeing that Donald never worked in television again. Donald said he'd like to think about it. He could imagine getting another job. He couldn't imagine never having a drink again.

A few days later, he told his boss he'd do it, and, on April 1st, less than two months before his 32nd birthday, Donald went into treatment. Barbara waited for him, with no money and three small children, alone in a cold new city.

*

Alcoholics build their lives on a tissue of lies that they tell themselves, Donald told me. It starts early, the lying. First the lies are an excuse, an explanation. But eventually the lies begin to define the alcoholic's character. In treatment, Donald was forced to confront and admit to the lies that he'd used to redefine himself, and then to deconstruct that person. He was asked to fearlessly examine himself. Fearlessly, Donald told me, is an important word.

In a setting where everyone harbored the same secret, where each person in the room was slowly disassembling that tissue of lies that was his life, Donald's own lies were not tolerated.

"Are you afraid of anything, Donald?" the group leader asked.

"No." The people in the group who had been in treatment a little longer than Donald smiled.

"You're not afraid of anything," the leader pressed.

"No, I'm not really afraid of anything," Donald said.

"Stop lying."

"I'm not lying."

"You need to leave the group now," the leader said.

"I have to finish treatment in order to get my job back."

"You'll never make it," the leader said, "because you are the worst liar I've ever heard. You can't waste the group's time any longer. Please leave."

"I've got to have this certificate or else I can't get my life back."

"You can't get your life back until you start telling the truth."

Donald begged the group leader to allow him to stay, and little by little, the people in the group began telling Donald what those truths were. Two weeks later, Donald had written a list that contained more than one hundred things that petrified him. At the top of that list was "failure." Donald was only worthy to himself if he was worthy to someone else. Whenever he drank, he didn't care whether or not he failed. For the periods of time when he was drunk, Donald said, he wasn't tortured. But drinking too much *guaranteed* his failure.

On May 27th, 1980, his 32nd birthday and 57th day sober, Donald says he died. The man who began his 32nd year—and his first—that day was my father.


I watch Sean gaze at the tiny television station. I know what he's thinking. He wants to be a television reporter too. When he gets back into the car, he says that it's amazing where one starts and where one ends up. Take your dad, for instance, he says. Yes, I agree, he is an amazing man.

After Donald got sober, his gifts were never again in question. He possesses three Emmy awards, a Columbia-DuPont citation, the Society of Professional Journalists award for service, and two Peabody awards.

But he started at this little brick box, and those awards were a long time coming, his decorations coming only after he'd crawled on his belly for many years. But all I ever knew of Donald was of "Dad"—hero, genius, saint. When I was ten years old, I asked my dad if he thought maybe he might be a reincarnation of Jesus Christ. He laughed and laughed but said nothing. He'd let me discover the answer myself.

Sean and I continue down the highway, and at the ocean the road splits. Barbara says to take a right on Middle Street and to look for an old stone church. If we arrive at Fort Moultrie, we've gone too far. We lurch to a stop at the intersection of Ben Sawyer and Middle Street. Directly across the crossroads, where The Gold Bug used to be, is a small box of a place called Dunleavy's Pub. When I tell Barbara about it later, she's crestfallen. Sean and I drive down Middle Street very slowly, looking for a small white house.

I remember seeing a picture of Donald sitting at the kitchen table in their pretty beach cottage. He has a blonde moustache and is smiling tenderly at Barbara's Irish Setter. The film picked up snatches of artificial light from an orange and green plastic lampshade. Directly below the lamp is a half-empty bottle of Jack Daniel's and two empty beer cans. It's a strangely comforting image. It's a picture of possibility, a picture of hope. Things can change. Things did.

Sean and I spot the cottage. It's a tiny beach cottage with side steps and the decaying remnants of a porch. I don't dare walk up to the front door but step out of the car. I stare through the windows of the house, through its halls and rooms. Sean reminds me that I wanted to take a black and white of the house for Barbara. I step onto the sidewalk and frame a photograph. As I steady the camera and look at the image of the house refracted against the lens, it looms at me like a flare. I am transported into the hallways and the kitchen, standing under the orange and green lampshade, staring my parents in the face. Lovely Barbara, not-yet-perfect Donald, the rivers they love and the children they dream of. I stand there on the sidewalk and draw in another breath before pressing the shutter. God splits time open like an apple and wedges in experiences like this one, I think as I snap the photograph.


Charleston is a peninsula made of rivers, carved by waters that have been moving toward the ocean for hundreds of thousands of years. But history is something more permanent, even than these two rivers, than this drop of land. It's something echoing inside you—gently at first, like the pluck of a single guitar string. It grows heavier, resounding in that place inside you insistently, until it becomes a bass drum in your chest. And you realize that you were here before, you knew these streets well, ate here, loved here. An incarnation of you memorized all the street names and waited at the docks to buy cheap crabmeat. I watched the boats off Sullivan's Island. I dreamed of children and felt my womb grow warm with possibility. Who was it on that beach, dipping her toes into the Atlantic Ocean? What screen door slammed shut on Middle Street, just a block from an old revolutionary sea fort? With increasing years, I'm allowed to view the dimmer parts of life before my name. It helped to find out that Golden wasn't always golden. That he drank sometimes, that he let people down sometimes. My jealousy, Dad always told me, was ignorant. Before I envy his success and his prizes, I should remember his shames and despair. It was suffered for me, ultimately, not in intent but in outcome. I am both of them—when darkness fell, Dad claimed fraternity. When dreams failed, Mom expressed hope. And I am a confluence of both rivers. ✧

# RECOMMENDATIONS

## POST ROAD

## RECOMMENDATION
# Ernest Hebert

John Griesemer

I'm going to go regional on you. I live in New Hampshire. This is the second time I've done that. The first time, some twenty-five years ago, I was working as a newspaper reporter, scuffling around to town meetings, school board confabs, traffic accidents, chimney fires, town fairs, and centenarians' birthdays. There was a paper down in the southern part of the state, in Keene, with a reporter who had a reputation for making good writing out of such truck. Ernie Hebert was his name. I never met the guy, but he was known as one of the best in our disparate and dissolute fraternity of New Hampshire news hounds.

Eventually, I left New Hampshire for New York City. Some years later I came across a glowing book review in the Sunday *New York Times* about a wonderful first novel, set in New Hampshire, written by Ernest Hebert. It took a few minutes of brain-wracking, but it came to me: this was the same Ernie Hebert. I had one of those moments when you see everything you've been doing in the bright light of someone else's achievements. Here was Ernie Hebert having written a novel that Anatole Broyard was saying gave him faith in the future of fiction. And here was I having...well, never mind.

But Broyard was right! I got the book and loved it. It had the power to cancel my envy and wounded pride and to make me just take pleasure in Hebert's accomplishment. Now, that's *some* writing. The book is *The Dogs of March,* and it's about as accurate a portrayal of the people who live up here in New Hampshire as you're going to find anywhere. Yes, this is the Granite State, and our blunt—or maybe blockheaded—motto is "Live Free or Die." The book explains why.

It's a simple enough tale. Howard Elman, a mill worker from the fictional town of Darby, NH, is struggling to hold his job and his family together, sometimes succeeding, sometimes doing an almost willfully botched job of it. Howard's biggest struggle is probably with his son who is the first in the family to attend college, but his most immediate and pressing problems are with his new neighbor from down country, a wealthy woman who wants his land. Holding that land becomes Howard's obsession, and he clings to it with the same intensity that the dogs of the title, run down and slaughter deer in the woods at the end of winter. There have been other books treading the same hardscrabble territory as *The Dogs of March.* But Hebert got here earlier and does it better.

And he's done it more. He's continued to write about the people of Darby and has completed four more novels *(A Little More Than Kin,*

*Whisper My Name, The Passion of Estelle Jordan* and *Live Free or Die*) set in the same region of southwestern New Hampshire. People draw comparisons to Yoknapatawpha, which is fine. But to put a more contemporary and rollicking spin on it, I'd say compare him and his work to William Kennedy and the rambunctiousness of his Albany novels.

It looked like Hebert could go on with Darby forever. But then, last year, he threw a change-up. He stayed pretty much in the same territory—near his native Keene—but he went back in time. Farther back than most American fiction goes. He went to the French and Indian War.

*The Old American* is a wonderful tale in the colonial tradition of "Indian captive" literature. Hebert grew up in Keene near the site of the house built by Nathan Blake, an English settler who was kidnapped by the Algonquins, lived with them for years as a slave, worked his way out of bondage, married into the tribe and only returned to white society when his English wife paid his ransom.

The narrative stroke that makes *The Old American* so fascinating is that Hebert tells the Nathan Blake story from the point of view of his Indian capturer, the "old American," Caucus Meteor. Garrulous, shrewd, stubborn, and a mystic who, in old age, must face his own mortality, Caucus Meteor grapples with his slave's clever orneriness and with the tribal infighting and desperation that grows as white settlers—both French and English—begin to exert the fatal pressure of their civilizations on the Indians.

Hebert makes this distant and little-understood moment in our continent's history as alive and vital as the stories he tells of modern Darby. Yes, they are regional novels. And, like good ones, they are universal. Hebert is spinning a cycle of stories of people and the land that is visionary and centuries long. ✧

# Recommended Reading

Julia Alvarez

For the four years in which I was busy researching and writing my last novel, *In the Name of Salomé,* most of my "extra" time was spent doing research for the book. Believe me, I wouldn't want to recommend all those thick historical tomes (many of them in Spanish) to anyone, not to mention books on everything from the history of dance to a study of building materials in the late nineteenth century to a manual full of treatments used for sufferers of TB. I admit some of this research reading was fun, but I often had to plow through a lot of facts and figures before finding the salient tidbit glinting like the proverbial needle in a haystack.

But I also read some wonderful books, all of them in the guise of research. Often, these books did help me learn something about a period in history or a certain technical aspect of writing with which I didn't feel confident. (How do I get a nineteenth-century woman in and out of her clothes?) Some of the things I learned from these books don't even show in my own. But what was most important was that the books below, which I approached as texts to teach me something, swept me into their narrative and carried me away. I forgot that I was reading with "a purpose" in mind and instead found myself reading for the best reason going: reading for sheer pleasure and the added bonus of expansion of the mind and spirit.

• Ha Jin, *Waiting:* I went to this novel to learn to "do" the texture of another culture, its details and flavors. Not only did I get immersed in Ha Jin's China, but I became totally caught up in this story of love and longing in a political minefield.

• Michael Cunningham, *The Hours*: I picked up this novel when I heard that Virginia Woolf was one of the main characters. Since I was also writing from the point of view of a famous writer, Salomé Ureña, I wanted to see how one of my favorite novelists dealt with some of the thorny issues of representation of a known figure. This elegant, beautifully crafted book is a continual flash of insight and fine writing. I wrote so many "keeper" passages in my journal, I finally abandoned this foolish transcription and instead put *The Hours* next to my *Websters* as a reference text.

• Janet Fitch, *White Oleander*: This gorgeously written book about the ambivalent and shifting relationship between a daughter and her poet-mother helped me in my own musings about Camila and her mother Salomé. I've since purchased several copies as gifts to my sisters and friends.

• Mayra Montero, *In the Palm of Darkness*: Though this novel's subject (search for a rare breed of frog by a North American herpetologist with the help of his Haitian guide) had nothing to do with my own, I wanted to immerse myself in the writing of a Caribbean author and live inside the imagery of the world. Montero's novel is enchanting and beautifully constructed. I learned a lot about using a dual point of view and tons about frogs!

• Alessandro Baricco, *Silk*: I bought this book on the recommendation of my sister Tita, who told me it was a mix between a love story, a historical novel, and a poem. Wow! I thought. I'm trying to do that, too. So I read *Silk* and I had to agree with Tita. A love story with a historical backdrop in the French silk trade, *Silk* is magical, shimmering and exquisite, like the fabric its hero journeys to acquire and the intriguing love he finds instead.

• Sebastian Faulkes, *Birdsong*: It does seem odd to go to a book written by a man to find out how a woman from earlier in the century might undress. This totally absorbing historical novel is like a first-world-war *Gone with the Wind*. What I admire so much about Faulkes is how none of his research "shows". . . well, maybe the tunnel-digging scenes. . . but they were so scary and exciting, I didn't care.

• Lahiri Jhumpa, *Interpreter of Maladies*: These stories, many of them about immigrants from India shuttling back and forth between cultures and states of mind, returned me to the honest and small details that convey marginality or multiculturalism in a character. What fun to discover a wonderful young writer with so many stories and novels ahead of her, which I'll get to read!

• J.M. Coetzee, *Disgrace*: I am ashamed to confess that it has taken me until this late in my reading life to have "discovered" a great writer who has been around for a while and about whom I always heard such high praise. I initially picked up this novel in order to learn how a white novelist might deal with representations of another race. I found much more: a new favorite writer! Fierce and spare—not an extra word or fuzzy or dishonest insight, Coetzee's writing has set a new standard for me as a writer. I've been reading everything I can get my hands on by him and have not been disappointed, though *Disgrace* is still the favorite by the favorite. But all his books I've read so far have been more than worth reading: *Waiting for the Barbarians, Boyhood,* and *Life and Times of Michael K,* and a book of essays, *Giving Offense.*

• Ishiguro Kazuo, *A Pale View of Hills*: How do we live with the burden of the past on our conscience? I was struggling with this question in my own novel. But I admit that I would read anything by Kazuo even without a "reason" or purpose in mind. I was captivated by this delicate, elliptical novel that taught me so much about the burden of surviving historical and personal tragedies. *The Remains of the Day* and *An Artist of the Floating World* are not bad either!

• Frederick Dillen, *Hero*: My wonderful editor, Shannon Ravenel, sent me to read this sharp-eyed, witty novel in order to help me get inside the head of a character who is reserved, ordinary, in some ways, not "your typical hero." Set in a restaurant with a multicultural cast of waiters, I enjoyed this novel so much that I was pleased to learn from Shannon that Algonquin had just published Dillen's second novel, *Fool*, which I have not yet read.

I have to slip in a poetry book! Often when I am working on prose, the flood of words is overwhelming. I want to stop and "dwell in possibility, a fairer house than prose," as Miss Emily calls poetry. Because she lived about the same time and was as rets—Wild Nights!" and "I cannot live with you" and "This is my letter to the world." If Salomé had written her "personal poems" in English they would have sounded a lot like Miss Emily's poems. ✧

# Mary Morrissey, Olena Kalytiak Davis, and Marisa de los Santos

Julianna Baggott

I have trouble reading for pleasure anymore. I've been told it's an occupational hazard, a cruel, ironic twist to being a writer. More often than not, I read with a rising panic, more the way one reads a map on I-95 on the way into Philly, past lit smokestacks and scrap-metal yards, looking for the route to the hospital where someone you love may be dying. Worse, the car is a convertible, the map all bird and violent wing-flap in your lap. I read because I've written myself into a corner, or because I haven't written anything at all, or because I want to remind myself that writing is worthwhile, a necessary joy.

And sometimes, when least expected, the pleasure of reading creeps up on me. No, more accurately, there is a book that refuses to be read like a map, refuses to be read with panic. And, suddenly, it's not only pleasure, but love. I fall in love with characters, sentences, words. Here are three recent romances.

My husband picked this book off the shelf off an editor's bookcase at Random House UK: Mary Morrissey's *Mother of Pearl* (not to be confused with the Oprah pick, by the same title). I started to read this book specifically for language. In the first few sentences, it became clear that the words themselves were going to be the most important event, and so I began underlining those that struck me, but by page three, I was transported. Morrissey is not only a genius within each sentence, she is a master of character and structure.

Olena Kalytiak Davis, author of *And Her Soul Out of Nothing*, a collection of poems, has an absolutely unique voice, a wild, philosophical mind. I find her astounding, poem after poem. I think she confounds and illuminates, breathtakingly.

Marisa de los Santos's collection *From the Bones Out* is precise and achingly beautiful. It is sweeping in its breadth, in what it takes on. The themes emerge and wind throughout the book, taking on one form and then another.

These three books make me jealous and desirous. They leave me tender. Proceed cautiously. ✧

RECOMMENDATION
# THE MEMORY ROOM by Mary Rakow

Janet Fitch

I see a lot of first novels. For some reason, publishers think "first novels" are a genre. Why first novels should have any more in common than fourth novels beats the hell out of me. Usually a first novel means three more in the drawer anyway, but the idea still holds. I should review first novels, because I am a first novelist (not counting the three in the drawer).

This is tough because I could care less about first novels. I want to read great novels, and could give a damn what their birth order is. I read a lot of charming (to somebody) first novels and stop half way (sometimes not even that) and go, 'What the hell do I care about this?' I don't want to be jollied, I don't want to be charmed. I want to be torn to pieces. I want to be struck dumb with admiration. And Mary Rakow does both in her first novel, *The Memory Room.*

A novel in verse form along the lines of William Carlos Williams' *Paterson* or Jabes' *The Book of Questions,* it is: jaw-droppingly ambitious, terrifying, grief-stricken, transcendent. Like the flight of bumblebees, it defies gravity, it defies likelihood, and yet, there it is. *The Memory Room* addresses the fundamental paradox of the existence of evil in a world created by God. Its protagonist, Barbara, a professor at a Catholic seminary, takes a leave of absence after a panic attack in a stuck elevator, and we watch her unravel, layer by layer, as fragments of a horrific childhood appear and won't be surpressed by her dozens of obsessive rituals. At last, she turns and, with the help of a subtle and sensitive therapist, opens the door to the room of memory.

This is not Sybil, or even *The Three Faces of Eve,* not an 'abuse book' or even a 'therapy book.' This is a work of art. It is no accident that Barbara uses as her thematic touchstone the work of Paul Celan, another survivor who forced himself to look directly into the face of evil and find the language to express it.

The book itself takes a musical structure, and music is a major element, both a source of solace and of pain, because it stirs memory, it stirs emotion. It is the spring rain which makes April the cruelest month. Art, and friendship, beauty and nature, all contain that duality, life stirring dangerously in the midst of void.

In reading this book, I felt the way I feel reading Li Young Lee's *The Winged Seed,* the purest of reader-joy, that someone could screen grief through such a fine sieve of language, and give us something so remorselessly beautiful. The big questions are asked by someone who knows where to find them, and knows these questions and not the horror of the incidents themselves, are the real meaning and salvation. ✧

# A GOOD HOUSE by Bonnie Burnard and BLINDNESS by José Saramango

Elizabeth Graver

I think of two novels I've read—and loved—over the past year. They're radically different from each other, yet each has strayed long in my mind. *A Good House*, by Canadian writer Bonnie Burnard, is the story of the Chambers family of Stonebrook, Ontario. Like a more conventional saga, it follows a family through several generations, but it does so in the calmest, most undramatic way, offering a subtle and intricate exploration of memory and forgetting, love and isolation, confluences and dispersals, all played out through this family's rather ordinary history. Burnard rarely comments, and she leaves it up to the reader to fill in much of the connective tissue between stories and to jump with her across time. You finish the book with a sense, almost, of having read an account of your own family history—some parts of it still blurry, some clearer, now, but all of it so dense, so ever-changing, that it has a kind of protean life of its own. The pacing—slow and steady—is brave, and the details are lingering and meticulous, revealing both what is luminous and what is distorted in everyday family life.

*Blindness*, by Portuguese Nobel Prize-winning writer José Saramango (translated by Giovanni Pontiero), is powerful in an entirely different way. The book takes place in a city stricken by a mysterious epidemic that renders people blind. It's an extended parable of sorts, deeply disturbing, yet not without some mitigating hope. Published in 1995, the novel nonetheless has a great deal to say about our post–September 11th era and what it means to live with fear, to respond to authority, to live compassionately, to survive, to act alone or in a group, to try to decipher a mysterious, often illogical world. Though this is, much more than Burnard's book, a novel of ideas, Saramango's rendering of the senses—and their loss—is full of poetry: "Here he was, plunged into a whiteness so luminous, so total, that it swallowed up rather than absorbed, not just the colours, but the very things and beings, thus making them twice as invisible." ✧

# THE CIRCUS OF DR. LAO by Charles G. Finney

Edward Hoagland

Just as, in a menagerie, some people will pause to marvel before the cage of an exotic creature from another hemisphere while others haul their children past, scarcely permitting them a glimpse, so, at the circus, some of us gasp at the trapezists' and the tumblers' feats, and other paying customers move restlessly in their seats and check their fingernails. In a circus we see mostly what we are ready to see. There is no script but chance and hope and spontaneity, and thus it is appropriate that this masterpiece of circus literature describes an imaginary circus, not a real one. No circus ought to be too "real."

Dr. Lao's stupendous show, which arrives abruptly in the Depression town of Abalone, Arizona, one hot August morning, introduces us to a hermaphrodite sphinx, a 2,300-year-old satyr, a lion-lizard-eagle dragon, and a gentle green hound, "less carnal than a tiger lily," with chlorophyll in its veins and a plait of ferns for a tail. Also, an angry sea serpent eighty feet long, whose one soft spot is for the circus mermaid; an ancient, intellectual magician who can bring men back from the dead; and a beautiful medusa who, with a glance, kills them.

Dr. Lao, the Chinese proprietor, travels with only three wagons and no roustabouts. Yet his numerous tents, black and glossy, stand about like darkened hard-boiled eggs on end. For such miraculous transformations he is indebted to his indispensable thaumaturge, Apollonius, who walks about "drowned in thought." Dr. Lao himself is energetic, impulsive, irascible, and resourceful—an impresario who, according to the emergencies of the moment, switches from the language of a poet-professor to the stock-comedy dialect of a Chinese laundryman "washing the smells out of shirttails," as two college boys, Slick Bromiezchski and Paul Conrad Gordon, put it to him.

The good doctor does have his troubles. The men in the crowd complain because the werewolf has turned into a woman three hundred years old, not the hot young dish they claim they were promised. A scientist who has examined his fearsome, enigmatic, phlegmatic medusa only wanted to identify the several species of snakes that constitute her hair (for which separate diets must be gathered). Circuses carry "a taint of evil or hysteria," Dr. Lao admits with regret. "Life sings a song of sex. Sex is the scream of life....Breed, breed, breed....Tumescence and ejaculation." One cause of his friend Apollonius's melancholy exhaustion is that things on the circus lot are forever getting out of hand—between the sea serpent and the dragon; between Satan and the witches who appear in the finale, some of them airsick from their flight to perform; between the bear (or is it a "Russian"?) and the mermaid it carries around the hippodrome; and between the satyr and Miss Agnes Birdsong, a high school English teacher who has come early in order to see the "Pan" that she observed driving a wagon during the opening parade through town.

Charles G. Finney, our cheerful author, was only thirty in 1935, when his *Circus* was published, so that his reactions are not the same as those of Apollonius, or even the "old-like, wealthy-looking party in golf pants" who represents Abalone's solidest citizens. At the time, Mr. Finney, a great-grandson of a famous Congregational divine who founded Oberlin College, was the veteran of a Missouri country boyhood, a year at the University of Missouri, and three years of garrison duty with Company E, Fifteenth U.S. Infantry Division, in Tientsin, China. An autodidact and intellectual rebel, he counted as his favorite twentieth-century writers Conrad, Kipling, Joyce, Proust, and Anatole France (but included no Americans). He had started the manuscript there in the army barracks in the American compound, writing in longhand, then laid it aside till he got home, because it had turned too lectury. Later, he dedicated the book to a soldier buddy in Tientsin, with whom he never crossed paths again.

Mr. Finney's sympathy for humdrum people and ordinary lives had a short fuse. Perhaps partly as a result, his book ran out of steam after ninety pages or so. When the delight and spontaneity begin to wane, we know the performance is almost over—not because of some inner novelistic logic but because, just as at a circus, the acts that he has brought to town have now all appeared, and it is simply *over*. In fact, the book's shortness probably explains why it is not better known, compared to bulkier underground classics, and why it needs reviving.

Wonders were what interested Finney—"real honest-to-goodness freaks that had been born of hysterical brains rather than diseased wombs," "the sports, the offthrows of the lust of the spheres," foaled from the earth, suggests the good doctor, the way the Surinam toad bears its offspring, through the skin of its back. Dr. Lao's perpetual, exasperated dither, the lassitude and the boredom of Apollonius, and the pell-mell terror of much of the show are the price of having a performance at all—which, for reasons unstated, of course must go on. ✧

# HEAD by William Tester

Tim Parrish

**M**y friend Geoff Schmidt turned me on to William Tester's *Head* (Sarabande, 2000) when I arrived at his house after a month on the road in a rental car (check out Schmidt's smart, sad, funny novel and spoof of how-to-write texts, *Write Your Heart Out: Advice from the Moon Winx Motel* on Smallmouth Press). When I finished *Head* the next day, I felt like a hard wind had blown right through me. Yeah, it blew me away. It went off like dynamite. It knocked me out. And it did it again when I read it in order to write this recommendation.

*Head* is a loose cycle of stories whose narrative spine is a group of chronologically reverted stories about the main character's (Nim) surviving a rough stepfather, a chaotic violent father, and a lot of sexual frustration. The rest of the stories seem to be the grown-up Nim bouncing around New York City and even Italy, the only exception being one story from the pointofview of a damaged Vietnam vet who could be Nim's father. Amy Hempel chose this book as the winner of the Mary McCarthy Prize in 1999, and at times I see similarities between Tester's and her aesthetics in their stories' fractured linearity and dense imagery. *Head*'s stories focus on writerly fascinations of mine—fear; sexuality; and the nature of masculinity in both the macho South and the modern urban world. But it's the language that made me curse and wow out loud both times I read the collection. Tester's sentences, his verbs, Jesus what verbs!, hit me the way Barry Hannah's, Mark Richard's, and Denis Johnson's hit me. It's like English blasted by a nuclear force and reassembled as something radioactive and stripped of nonessentials, even when the narrator is sorting for the right words himself. The language is both shards glinting and penetrating, and sentences so physical they throttle you, thump your heart, and lick along your funny bone. Sure, Tester's language will strike some as eccentric because it is eccentric, but it's stunning, too.

The narratives are also damn good. As I mentioned, fear lies at the core of almost all of them. Fear of lightning, of brutal men, of the unseen, of sexual discovery, of being controlled, of losing control. The stories range in content from the main character, his brother, and their step-dad in an aluminum boat and stringing barbed wire across a mucky lake during a lightning storm ("The sky turns a gray like the lack of good color, and the rain doesn't let up, but the weak are forgiven, and I know the absolute bomb is falling, or something like that, really big") to a young man tripping, drifting, and lusting in New York City ("She went in me, way up inside my mind, right there, our faces all lit up with wanting, clearly radiating light"). Like the second quoted line, many moments of illumination (often dark or unrequited) cause these characters to actually fill with light, and the stories earn this intensity without fail. In "The Living and the Dead," the narrator wakes in a muddy field "To a milk-white, hideous lightning" and "Blackness, a freezing and locust-like rain." The ground itself clutches him, ghosts threaten to pull him under until he jerks his foot free of his boot and feels "all washed and alive." Many of these stories hinge on moments of ambiguous aliveness, orgasms of disappointment, and losses of coupling. The stories give a painful sense of being a body, of skin laid bare so the nerves get it all, every bit. From "Cousins": "A churning curdles in my stomach, eases shuddery to calm...I imagine all the colors in the hollowness of her, inside her body, the tubing pipework of her blood, her netted stomach gourd in gray...She has her heart and lungs inside of her in darkness in her chest, and air is there somewhere as well, the liquid ball of light in Kay, and Jesus' face is in her, too...The air it jitters cues from Kay to me—and back from me, to her, like she knows what is doing in my head to do with her."

*Head* is an intimate, vulnerable, raw, beautiful, brilliant book. The writing is never predictable, even when the stories move into territory they themselves have predicted. Rather, the writing is often startling with its torqued language and severe disjunctions. Read it and see.  ✧

# The Memoir Bank

Michael Moon

Some people love True Crime books. Me, I prefer True Fiction, which is how I think of the memoir. Less closely focused on the day-to-day than the diary, less relentlessly inward than the journal, and (at least somewhat) less made up than most novels, the memoir provides its reader with a lifetime's, even an epoch's, worth of memories of splendor and misery, to be sorted through at leisure. If you are an omnivorous reader and worry sometimes about being able to maintain supply indefinitely, the memoir will never let you down. Consider laying in a basic stock, as well as some of the best current examples of the form. A good place to start: the memoirs of the Duc de Saint-Simon, an unlikely Scheherazade at the court of Louis XIV; the handsome and sturdy three-volume English translation by Lucy Norton is available in paperback at the Metropolitan Museum of Art's gift shop as well as from Amazon. Saint-Simon's preternatural nose for dish and his ability to follow a cast of hundreds through decades of feuds, amours, social triumphs, and humiliations inspired the most memoiristic of novelists, Proust.

Ulysses S. Grant wrote his memoirs as he was dying from oral cancer, hoping to shore up the family finances. Stoic and plainspoken, they have elicited the admiration of readers as different as Matthew Arnold and Gertrude Stein. Henry James penned a surpassingly charming memoir of his childhood, entitled *A Small Boy and Others*. James himself was addicted to the glamorous memoirs of the Napoleonic era, from the military adventures of the dashing Baron de Marbot to the courtly intrigues of the Duchess d'Abrantès, lady in waiting to the emperor's mother and a people-watcher so astute that Balzac took lessons from her. (With his domelike cranium full of the festivals and imbroglios of the First Empire, is it any wonder that Henry James in his deathbed delirium dictated letters in the person of Bonaparte himself?) Trapped at home without a good memoir on hand? Never fear; the internet is shaping up as a near-ideal purveyor of the form. Visit, for example, *www.napoleonic-literature.com*, which has on offer Marbot's memoirs in their entirety, as well as information on how to order such gems as a CD-ROM containing the complete memoirs of Madame de Rémusat, for ten dollars. Ask yourself, which are you really going to enjoy more and for longer, for the same amount of money, that new horny-teen pic at the multiplex around the corner, or the memoirs of La Rémusat?

Two memoirs published in 2000 attest to the current vigorous health of the genre. In ravishingly attentive prose, Kathleen Finneran's

*The Tender Land* tells the story of her family's struggles to come to terms with the suicide of her younger brother; the book was awarded a Whiting Prize this past year. Lee Martin, in *From Our House*, richly and soberly recalls what it was like growing up as an only child in the years after his father lost both his hands in a farming accident. More than content to be mesmerized by the sheer intensity and beauty of the writing in both books, I occasionally drew myself up as I read them to ponder how the process of writing itself can serve to extend memory to what seems like an almost superhuman degree: witness the ability of both Finneran and Martin to recall with hypnotic thoroughness family conversations and playground contretemps that took place thirty or forty years ago. ✧

# THE TRUE DETECTIVE by Theodore Weesner

Stewart O'Nan

Theodore Weesner is one of the very few American novelists to have written two great novels. His first novel, *The Car Thief*, is a magnificent and moving portrait of an unhappy teenager growing up in a bleak industrial city, told in prose that is mostly transparent yet contains lovely, seemingly effortless metaphors. Weesner's intimate realism is rewarding but requires some patience from the reader, and a willingness to inhabit his character Alex as fully as the author does—not quite the same patience and willingness Larry Woiwode asks of the reader in *Beyond the Bedroom Wall* and *Born Brothers*, but close. The depth Weesner summons from a character most people would see as flat or spent—the disaffected teen—is invigorating, as if every person around us might possess such a wealth of feeling.

From its publication in 1972, *The Car Thief* was recognized as a major novel. It spent time in the '80s as a Vintage Contemporary trade paperback, and is now available in a new edition from Grove. Not so *The True Detective*.

By 1987, when Summit published *The True Detective*, Weesner was an established author. After *The Car Thief*, he published a small second novel called *A German Affair*, which follows the romance of a young G.I. in the early '50s. The admirable intimacy Weesner creates is still in effect, but the book—perhaps because of its scope—isn't as satisfying as *The Car Thief*. There may not be enough at stake in *A German Affair*—the peril nothing more than personal disappointment, lost love. Like *The Car Thief*, this second novel is also mostly episodic, the story line energized only by the main character's personality, which in this case isn't as interesting or conflicted as Alex.

In *The True Detective*, Weesner swings the other way. Everything is at stake—life, limb, innocence, the moral fiber of the nation. In Portsmouth, New Hampshire, a confused young man kidnaps and sexually assaults a boy. One police lieutenant has the responsibility of finding the boy before it's too late, and also, for his own peace of mind, making sense of the crime. The kid goes missing, and the whole city becomes the stage. Weesner digs deep into the boy's mother and brother while the passing time cranks up the tension of his plot line.

These are the ingredients of a cop-and-robber thriller, except that Weesner's sense of complexity undercuts the melodrama. His portrait of the young man, Vernon, is amazingly empathetic without once excusing him for what he's doing, just as his look into Lieutenant Gil Dulac is generous yet never simply admiring. The two men are singled out, isolated in their hopes and fears, their hard-earned views of the world.

*The True Detective* is tough-minded, but subtly done. The language, the details, the progress of the POV sections—everything serves Weesner's total effect brilliantly. And while it deals with a sensational, even loaded subject, ultimately I'd say the novel is that rare achievement, a wise book, and maybe the saddest book I've read. That it's also a page-turner is a marvel.

And yet, *The True Detective* is out of print, and when people think of great American novelists, few think of Theodore Weesner. I won't waste time speculating on why this is. Find *The True Detective* (have your library interloan a copy or look it up on www.abebooks.com) and *The Car Thief* and see what he's up to. ✧

# AUNT JULIA AND THE SCRIPTWRITER
## by Mario Vargas Llosa

Tom Perrotta

It's easy to divide writers into neat categories based on the presence or absence of humor in their work—there are the funny ones (Evelyn Waugh, Thomas Berger, David Lodge), for whom the comic effect is often the highest priority; the serious ones (Virginia Woolf, Joyce Carol Oates, John Edgar Wideman) who rarely crack a smile; and the mongrels (Philip Roth, Lorrie Moore, Tobias Wolff) who find a way to consistently combine comedy and deep moral purpose in their work. More unusual are the switch hitters, serious writers who take an occasional break from their weighty concerns and cut loose with an unexpected romp (Jane Smiley's *Moo* comes to mind).

The great Peruvian novelist, Mario Vargas Llosa, is rightly celebrated for epic political novels like *The War of the End of the World, Conversation in the Cathedral,* and his latest, *The Feast of the Goat,* an ambitious and unflinching account of life in the Dominican Republic during the Trujillo era. The odd book out in the roster of Vargas Llosa's masterworks has to be *Aunt Julia and the Scriptwriter,* a manic farce about forbidden love and the dangerous power of storytelling that is a triumph of literary switch-hitting, and, quite simply, one of the funniest books I've ever read.

The novel alternates on a chapter-by-chapter basis between a fairly conventional bildungsroman (the story of Varguitas, an aspiring writer who falls in love with his beautiful aunt, as Vargas Llosa himself had done), and madcap recreations of soap operas written by the supremely talented and superhumanly prolific Pedro Camacho, the Balzac of Latin American radio ("He's not a man, he's an industry.... He writes all of the stage plays put on in Bolivia, and acts in all of them. And he also writes all the radio serials, directs them, and plays the male lead in every one of them.") As Varguitas plunges deeper into his passionate affair with Aunt Julia, Pedro Camacho's stories begin spinning out of control. Dead characters inexplicably return to life. Living ones appear in the wrong programs, or indulge in inappropriate and sometimes shocking behavior (a priest rewards his young male students by handing out pornographic pictures, and teaches the young girls "how to pad out their breasts, hips and bottoms with cotton, pillows, and even newspapers, how to do the dances that were the latest rage: the rumba, the  huaracha, the porro, the mambo.") Even worse, Camacho peppers his scripts with gratuitous swipes at Argentina, a country he despises with fanatical fervor ("I've killed my own daughter," one character laments. "The only thing left to do is go live in Buenos Aires.") In the end, poor Camacho goes completely mad, and Varguitas learns the prices to be paid for loving the wrong woman and risking a career in literature.

It's hard to do justice to the sheer energy and inventiveness of this novel in a brief summary—it's as if Vargas Llosa somehow figured out a way to channel the primal storytelling powers of Pedro Camacho while he was composing *Aunt Julia and the Scriptwriter*. As a result, one of the world's preeminent political novelists managed to transform himself, for this book, and this book alone, into a fabulous and wickedly transgressive comic writer. ✧

# THE HOLY BIBLE: KING JAMES VERSION

Mary Sullivan

The Bible is sanctum; the world, sputum.
*—Franz Kafka*

**S**ex, violence, treason, deception, incest, bestiality, circumcision, butchery, love, beauty, poetry, humor, hope, redemption, and the promise of life everlasting: it's all here. The story is simple enough: God creates the earth and man; man falls into sin; God makes a covenant with His chosen people, but they betray him; God sacrifices His only son Jesus Christ to save man from his sins. As Jesus overcomes death and lives forever, so can man if he is baptized and believes. In his final chapters, John writes:

> This is the disciple which testifieth of these things, and wrote these things:
> And we know that his testimony is true.
> And there are also many other things which Jesus did, the which, if they should be written, every one, I suppose that event the world itself could not contain the books that should be written. Amen.
> (John 21:24-25)

There are infinite stories left unsaid and unwritten, that the "world itself could not contain the books that should be written." Likewise there are infinite possibilities of what is left open to interpretation. For the individual books that make up the Bible were written over a period of more than 1,000 years by many different authors. The word "Bible" comes from a plural Greek word, "ta Biblia," which means "the little scrolls." In all its various forms—prose, poetry, parables, legal codes, proverbs, maxims, and riddles—the Bible is a whole, which speaks best for itself.

The language and style of the Bible ranges from the mundane to the beautiful:

> You are dust, and to dust you shall return. (Genesis 3:19)

> I am Who I am. (Exodus 3:14)

> Thou shalt not suffer a witch to live. (Exodus 3:4)

> And if a man lie with a beast, he shall surely be put to death: and ye shall slay the beast. (Leviticus 20:15)

He that spareth his rod, hateth his son: but he that loveth him chasteneth him betimes. (Proverbs 13:24)

A dog returneth to his vomit, so a fool returneth to his folly. (Proverbs 26:11)

Let him kiss me with the kisses of his mouth: for my love is better than wine. (Song of Solomon 1:2)

Do not throw your pearls before swine. (Matthew 7:6)

Knowledge puffs up, but love builds up. (Corinthians 8:1)

This is my commandment, that ye love one another. (John 15:12)

Some of the simple parables are written in the most powerful language, as when David, "armed with the name of the Lord" kills Goliath.

And David put his hand in his bag, and took thence a stone and slang it, and smote the Philistines in the forehead, that the stone sunk into his forehead, and he fell to the earth. (1 Samuel 17:49)

Much of the Old Testament slogs through pages of laws, genealogies, and lengthy descriptions on how to build the ark of the covenant or a temple (this can be amusing if one is reading out loud with someone, as I did with my husband). Then there are lines that read beautifully purely for their sound or descriptive detail:

A golden bell and a pomegranate, a golden bell and a pomegranate, upon the hem of a robe round about. (Exodus 28:34)

Or for their repetition, rhythm, and metaphors:

Vanity of vanities, saith the Preachers, vanity of vanities; all is vanity. (Ecclesiastes 1:2)

My days are swifter than the weaver's shuttle. (Job 7:6)

My beloved is like a roe or a young hart. (Song of Solomon 2:9)

Or for their pathos and despair:

Oh my son Absalom, my son, my son Absalom! Would God I had died for thee, O Absalom, my son, my son! (2 Samuel 18:21)

How long will ye vex my soul, and break me in pieces with words? (Job 2:19)

My God, my God, why have you forsaken me? (Matthew 27:46)

As Ecclesiastes tells us, even the best life is limited in knowledge, virtue, and power. In the face of vanity and death, "There is nothing better for a man than that he should eat and drink, and that he should make his soul enjoy good in his labor," (Ecclesiastes 2:24). The Bible offers wisdom, hope, and redemption for all us sinners. We can let the world slide, but as Kafka says, the word of the Bible is "sanctum." ✧

# THE MASSACHUSETTS REVIEW

LEONARD BASKIN

A QUARTERLY REVIEW *of* Fiction, Poetry, Essays, and Art, *since 1959*
*single copy*: $8 ($11 *International*)
Subscriptions: 1 Year $22; 2 Years: $34; 3 Years $52

**The Massachusetts Review**

*editorial office*: South College, University of Massachusetts, Amherst, MA 01003 ph: 413-545-2689
e: massrev@external.umass.edu • www.massreview.org

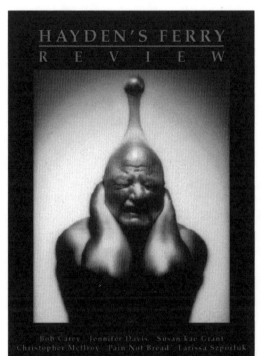

# BENNINGTON WRITING SEMINARS

*MFA in Writing and Literature*
*Two-Year Low-Residency Program*

A. BLAKE GARDNER

## FICTION
## NONFICTION
## POETRY

Scholarships available

For more information contact:
Writing Seminars, Box AG
Bennington College
Bennington, VT 05201
802-440-4452
Fax 802-440-4453
www.bennington.edu

# Jonathan Lethem

Jonathan Lethem is the author of the novels *Gun, With Occasional Music;
Amnesia Moon; As She Climbed Across the Table; Girl in Landscape;
Motherless Brooklyn;* and *The Shape We're In.* He is also the author of one
collection, *The Wall of the Sky, the Wall of the Eye.* He lives in Brooklyn.

**POST ROAD:** I read somewhere that you were an art student at
Bennington College. What kind of art and what were your years at
Bennington like?

**JONATHAN LETHEM:** I painted because my father painted, and I painted badly because it wasn't really what I wanted to do. But it took a while to
work that out. My dad's spent his life an artist of tremendous dedication,
worked steadily in a variety of styles and mediums—though primarily oil-
on-canvas—always exploring, always faithful to his gift. Which he
unearthed against certain odds, being raised in the Midwest the son of a
traveling salesman of agricultural supplies, in a large, mostly conservative
family that doesn't boast another artist (though there was one writer). I
inherited a portion of his facility without thinking twice about it—and
also the whole legacy of his and my mother's bravely-constructed
bohemian, radical, and 'artistic' lifestyle as though it were the only possible way to live. The facility for drawing and painting turned out, once I'd
discarded it, to be a tease, or distraction, on the way to something else.
The wider background—lifestyle, cultural literacy, home-schooling in
dedication, craft, everyday work—made me a writer.

But I painted for a while, using my inherited eye and hand. I went to
Music and Art, the great New York high school, which turned out Harvey
Kurtzman, Milton Glaser, Erica Jong, Bess Myerson among other mostly
Jewish notables. My work was glib, show-offy, usually cartoonish. The
most serious attempts were loaded with narrative implications, a struggling against wall art's inability to depict time. By the time I was fifteen I'd
already made an animated film and written a 125-page 'novel'—in other
words, on the side, I was pushing against painting in forms that better
contained my feeling for story. But by following my father as a painter I
was telling another story, one I couldn't give up yet. So when I applied to
Bennington it was as a prospective art student, with a portfolio.

There I degenerated quickly. Because I'd been an art student for four
years already, and lived in my dad's household, I considered myself too good
for the introductory classes. A teacher named Guy Goodwin saw through
me. He wrote an evaluation which praised the talent I'd exhibited in the
tossed-off work, and was nominally a high passing grade—at Bennington
there were only written evaluations—but concluded by mentioning. I'd

barely even been a participant in the class. He doubted I'd be an artist.

Midway through freshman year I began another novel, called *Apes In the Plan*, after a line from a Devo song. With that, the painting was finished in any meaningful sense, though since I was still mired in a dilettantish career as a student I took a few more art classes and made some more half-assed art. Shortly after that I dropped out of Bennington. My experience there was overwhelming, mostly having to do with a collision with the realities of class—my parents' bohemian milieu had kept me from understanding, even a little, that we were poor. I've written about this a bit in an essay for *Tin House* called "Defending The Searchers," and discussed it with Phillip Lopate and Dalton Conley in an interview for *Salon*. It's an endlessly fascinating subject for me—the oddity of being raised in a hipster fog where intellectualism and cultural access obscured poverty so completely it became a kind of privilege. Partly a New York experience, and partly a sixties-seventies thing. I thought I was one of the chosen ones. But at Bennington that was all demolished by an encounter with the fact of real privilege. I couldn't have articulated this at the time, but within a year there my sunny sense of boho destiny was transformed into surly outsider-underclass resentment, an artist's identity which was simultaneous self-loathing and arrogant. I was shocked, shocked, to discover that a large number of artistic careers are essentially purchased, and Bennington was implicated in this awakening. I spun out, unable to continue there, to make use of what was, in fact, being offered. Even so, the year-and-a-half I spent was hugely influential, and some of my teachers and fellow students made me aware of standards I still measure myself against. Paradoxical, how much influence could be imparted by a place I seemed to be rejecting almost as soon as I set foot in it. Like a family experience, I guess.

**PR:** You were for a time the fiction editor of *Fence*. What role do literary magazines play in the national discussion of art and literature?

**JL:** Tough for me to generalize in any way that doesn't seem completely windy. I was fiction editor of *Fence* for six issues, and I tried to make the fiction we published there unexpected—because I began by publishing only four stories a year, I had to make it really unexpected to make it anything at all. Under Rebecca Wolff's genius stewardship, the magazine has become an important one in the poetry world, which is what I think it was devised for, really. The fiction existed in a blessed 'free-zone'—by reversing the usual proportion the fiction was turned into the kind of unexpected-and-possibly-irrelevant fugitive stuff that poetry usually is in a magazine full of fiction and articles. I think in those six issues we (there were talented readers helping me) might have made a couple of nice discoveries, or anyway been the second or third publication for some writers who were about to turn heads. I just don't know what to say about a role in the culture. Each story or poem or book gropes for a role or at least a walk-on in the heads of individual readers or listeners. It was fun to be the head doing the choosing, for a while.

**PR:** Is there a distinction in your mind between literary and commercial fiction? Or have we been trained to think in those terms by the national chains of bookstores?

**JL:** Hmm. There's a gulf nimbly skipped over in those two questions, in the distance between 'in your mind' and 'trained by national chains'. I've spent a lot of energy arguing to myself and to others that certain books I love are a much more interesting part of the 'literary' conversation for anyone who troubles to read them than they're usually regarded to be (by bookstores, chains, critics, various canon-making entities). On the other hand, if I pick up the sort of book I don't usually bother to pick up and find it unsurprisingly uninteresting, I'm as quick to label it 'commercial' as anyone. It's a useful dismissal.

**PR:** Is the decision to marry traditional genres of fiction with a more literary bent an external one? Or does the material lend itself one way or the other?

**JL:** Things get really confusing when you bring in the word genre as if everyone understands what it means. In my view, the words which name bookstore sections (and reviewing and publishing categories) describe clusters of genres—and that includes the bookstore section called 'fiction' or 'literature'. Novels obedient and disobedient to the conventions of various definable and specific genres like 'the campus novel', 'the bildungsroman', the 'hard-boiled detective novel', 'the family romance', 'the epic quest', 'the dystopian social novel', 'the paranoid noir' 'the gothic tale', 'the epistolary romance', 'the ghost story' and many others nestle within those big, broad, and nearly meaningless (meaningless, anyway, within any really interesting critical or 'literary' conversation) categories like mystery or fiction or science fiction or literature or romance.

But I'm pontificating. But your question invited me to pontificate. But I'm not really liking hearing myself pontificate. So I'll take the easy out: I'm personally not much interested in these dissections anymore. Taxonomy thrives on dead subjects. I'm always more thrilled by fiction which is disobedient to the genre conventions with which it engages, and by fiction which engages simultaneously with more than one genre or mode or set of expectations.

And for me the material always dictates form. Ever more so as I've grown as a writer.

**PR:** *Motherless Brooklyn* has been described as a literary detective novel.

What in your mind separates your novel from the detective novels of Ross Macdonald and Agatha Christie and others who have written books in the detective and mystery genre?

**JL:** From Agatha Christie, only everything. Ross Macdonald, like Raymond Chandler, was a central influence on *Gun, With Occasional Music*, and so of course he's humming away underneath my second attack on the hard-boiled conventions in *Motherless*. But unlike Chandler, I haven't reread MacDonald in fifteen years, so I'd have difficulty isolating his relevance to the more recent book.

As I've crankily suggested in my reply to your earlier question, I'm responding to individual writers always, whole genres never. Why argue with a cloud? The only other hard-boiled writers who matter to me as much as MacDonald and Chandler—and none matter as much as those two—are Crumley, Hammett, and the very early Ellroy. The other stuff that's shelved in mystery sections which I care about isn't the harmless cheery crime-solving Agatha Christie stuff, it's the much more erratic and vivid 'crime novel' (defined by the presence of a criminal protagonist): Goodis, Thompson, Willeford, Cain, McCoy.

**PR:** In choosing Lionel Essrog, who is afflicted with Tourette's Syndrome, as the narrator of *Motherless Brooklyn*, you provide an excellent trope for breaking the mold of the traditional detective novel, a trope that allows the novel to also be about language and how language is processed in the human mind. Which came first—the decision to have a Tourettic narrator or the idea of writing a detective story? And how did you go about researching Tourette's? What was the decision process in giving the narrator this affliction over any other kind of affliction?

**JL:** They came together. I'd been gathering interest in and material about Tourette's half-consciously, reading Oliver Sacks and watching a documentary called "Twitch and Shout" and becoming responsive to the material in ways I couldn't explain. I saw something of myself in Tourette's, particularly in certain verbal inversions and reworkings and free-associatings which I'd manifested in controlled ways in my earlier fiction. Because Tourette's is always about expulsiveness *restrained*. The attempt to put boundaries or controls or explanations around the irrational, explosive expression. I saw I'd allowed this impulse in my work by a series of Tourettish characters: the babyheads in *Gun*, the blind guys in *As She Climbed*, and certainly the Archbuilders in *Girl in Landscape*. Always these characters were delightful screwballs working the margins of the narrative—I kept them restricted, like a Greek chorus of Shakespearean fools. So learning about Tourette's itself became an incitement to loosen up this part of my work, give it freer play.

But I didn't know I could write about Tourette's until my curiosity about the syndrome floated into range of my long-standing annoyed-admiring feeling for the hard-boiled narrator. Just as I never imagined I'd again have anything to say in the hard-boiled voice (after *Gun*) until the idea of the Tourettic detective arrived. The two activated one another, and I knew it was a book. (I should add as an aside that at first I meant Lionel to be a 'real' detective, then realized just how untenable I believe a contemporary hard-boiled detective to be. He had to become a fake, and this question — how really stupid and unworkable the Chandler impulse is in a contemporary setting — invested in the book.)

Of course I found it incredibly funny, snort-milk-through-the-nose funny. I still do. As much as I've invested in Lionel and his Tourette's— and he's obviously the character I've written with whom I most identify —it all starts with wanting to do this funny, stupid, seemingly impossible thing. Subsequently, I layered over the potential affront of how funny I wanted to be with all kinds of intricate sensitivity to the real-world suffering of Touretters and their loved ones. It's an affliction—in the lives of sufferers and their families often a terrible one. And the world is terribly insensitive. I didn't want to add to that even slightly. I hope I haven't. But the book in fact thrived on this struggle to have things both ways—my awkward negotiation translated to the reader, I think, so that it becomes a very emotional book, very emotionally open.

**PR:** Two of the characters in *Motherless Brooklyn*, the bookkeeper Ullman, and Gilbert, are off-camera for most of the novel. How did your decision to manage the characters on the page evolve? Was the hierarchy of the four—Essrog, Tony, Danny, and Gilbert—immediately clear to you? You've said previously that Lionel was to be the main character from the start, but how did you build the other characters?

**JL:** Well, I'm embarrassed by both explanations in different ways. Ullman is a "No Man" or "All Men" (but not Allman Brother) type of thing, and he was never meant to appear. A fucking intentional symbol, that's what I'm confessing. As for Gilbert, I bungled into that problem. I needed a second Minna Man in the car with Lionel at the start, and I'd intended him to be an 'extra' type—one who could be killed off or jailed and forgotten while the other 'important' Minna Men were back at the ranch. I probably should have guessed that after fifty pages of banter, he and Lionel would start to seem inseparable in a Mutt-and-Jeff kind of way. So, managing his absence became one of those damage-control aspects of writing the book. But maybe it worked out okay. The book is intentionally structured around an unbearable breach—Minna's vanishing. And then Gilbert becomes a little bit of an anodyne to that loss, a pothole instead of a bottomless well of grief: "See, some people go away and come back. Rescue isn't completely hopeless," etc.

Tony was essential from the start. Should I say he's based on a kid I knew? Um, several real-life sources, cough, cough. Danny was more filler.

I mean, I knew he had to be somebody fun and interesting (in fact I ended up borrowing from the future, just like George W. Bush does—Danny's white-blackness is a foreshadowing of my current work). I just didn't know how he'd be essential to the book. But when you're lucky, as I was in several ways during this writing, everything has its purpose. I had no inkling Danny was destined to inherit the agency until I got to the last chapter, but it seems obvious now, doesn't it?

PR: In *As She Climbed Across the Table,* you send up academia, and the absurdities of that small, self-sustaining world. At one point, Georges De Tooth, the resident deconstructionist, pitches his proposal to study Lack, the hole in the universe opened up by Professor Soft, saying "Physics seeks to dismantle the surface, perceive beyond it, to a truth comprised of particles; I argue against depth wherever I find it. Lack's meaning is all on the surface..." Extrapolated, the above could apply to literary criticism. What is your opinion of the business of literary criticism, and further, is there anything writers can learn from literary criticism of their work?
JL: Of course. Defensiveness requires writers (including myself) say otherwise, constantly, but of course. It just has to be very good literary criticism, which is as rare as other kinds of good stuff—writing, cooking, conversation. And what's handy with criticism—academic and 'popular'—is that the bad parodies itself.

PR: Another aspect of *As She Climbed Across the Table* is an evolution of the Koan about one hand clapping, in the form of the twin blind men, Garth and Evan, who propose a new theory on perception, that true perception comes from within and not from without (an idea another character, Dawn, espouses in *Amnesia Moon*). How did the germ of this idea begin, and how did you conceive of Garth and Evan to carry the idea in the novel?
JL: Subjectivity isn't a new theory of perception. You're flattering me by taking it backwards, as though the ideas were profound and the characters mere vehicles. In fact the only thing interesting about that talk is that it carries with it the flavor of the particular invention—Dawn and the two blind guys have charm, so they've persuaded you to *feel* something about an otherwise banal observation. I think. Anyway, they were hardly conceived as a vehicle. I just saw them one day: two borderline-autistic blind guys, very poetic, one black, one white, with a wonderful pataphysical rap. Then they needed to have something to say, so I pillaged Borges and *Rashamon.* That's all.

PR: How did the idea of writing a narrative around Lack manifest in your mind? Does Lack have kin in Contemporary American Fiction?
JL: He sure does. His twin is the narrator of John Barth's *End of the Road,*

a novel which obsessed me. Barth's book is told from the point of view of an inert and diffident character who steals away the wife of a dynamic professorial blowhard. The professor is appalled to lose in a romantic triangle to a cipher, a void. So, I made the void literal and shifted the viewpoint. And then made the whole thing cuddly, and more contemporary and Delillo-ish. Though now that I think about it, if you know the Barth, it makes the 'cold steel table' aspect of my book a little bit yucky.

**PR:** In *Amnesia Moon* the entire world is not what or where it should be, yet one constant is the presence of televangelists (from all faiths) and the indifferent masses. What were you trying to say about religion in the book?

**JL:** I have to keep flipping these questions around. The televangelist robots came first, as an image, as a joke, as a Philip K. Dick-ian riff on the mechanization and co-modification of, well, anything passionate, anything native and human. I think—this was a long time ago—that I was mostly just making fun of the word 'televangelist'. It was funny and made me picture these robots with television heads and babbling religious leaders on the screens of the televisions. I wanted my character to meet one of these things.

**PR:** Toward the end of *Amnesia Moon*, the residents of Vacaville have their appearance altered to pale in comparison to those of the "government stars," who are more beautiful than the average person (so much so that residents can only buy *Playboy* according to their body type). What is your opinion of the tyranny of beauty in our culture as perpetuated by the media, etc.?

**JL:** Much what you'd imagine. It's awful. But it's awful because it preys on and interfaces with all sorts of horrible Darwinianly hardwired body instincts. It just milks them to death. But again, I was only trying to be funny. That scene with the porn is like a rebus. Like a Jenny Holzer billboard, or a Laurie Anderson song. There's an opinion in there, but it's not my own. The scene is built on the foundation of a cultural critique just about every second person in Berkeley in 1987 (which is where I was when I wrote it) was already walking around with, fully formed, in their head. It becomes amusing to see the common understanding gimmicked into a little artistic rebus of that kind—the pleasure is in the recognition. If I claimed to have originated those observations I'd be a madman.

**PR:** Do you have favorite books that you read over and over?

**JL:** Sure. There's no sense to them as a grouping, I suspect. Just talismans, singular objects, some or all flawed, which keep me going, like friends. Some novels: James Salter's *Light Years*. Shirley Jackson's *The*

*Road Through the Wall.* Christina Stead's *The Man Who Loved Children.* Philip K. Dick's *Ubik.* John Barth's *End of the Road.* Patricia Highsmith's *The Cry of the Owl.* James Baldwin's *Another Country.* Don Delillo's *White Noise.* Robert Heinlein's *Door Into Summer.* E.M. Forster's *A Passage to India.* Parts of Samuel Delany's *Dhalgren.* And certain stories by Italo Calvino ("All At One Point," "The Dinosaurs," "The Aquatic Uncle"), Frank O'Connor ("My Oedipus Complex," "Man of the House"), James Thurber ("The Catbird Seat," "The Wood Duck," "One Is A Wanderer") and others. But really none of those compares with the small group of children's books I've read many dozens of times: Lewis Carroll's *Alice* books, Norton Juster's *Phantom Tollbooth,* Eric Berne's *The Happy Valley,* Dr. Seuss's *Sleep Book,* Albert Payson Terhune's *His Dog.* Or, honestly, certain books of music writing I've read hundreds of times. A collection of essays edited by Greil Marcus called *Stranded*—I re-read half that book every time I pick it up, I lose whole days to it, I have to hide it from myself in my house, like porn.

**PR:** What was your experience with publishing your first book, *Gun, With Occasional Music?*

**JL:** That experience was delirious. I was paid six thousand dollars by Harcourt Brace. My editor had worked with Stanislaw Lem and Umberto Eco. And he showed it to another editor in the house, an 'old hand', who said my overtly Chandler-esque prose wasn't an insult to Chandler. I'd pictured my first novels being published as paperback originals and instead a prestigious house was doing the book in cloth. And then they allowed me to art-direct the jacket design, which I arranged to look as much like a paperback original as possible. I was in heaven. This euphoria carried me a certain distance, then I began to want to make a living.

**PR:** What are some artistic influences on you outside of the world of books?

**JL:** Shamelessly fun ones. Film—Hawks, Ford, Hitchcock, Welles, Truffaut, Kubrick and Godard above all. Plus Warner Brothers cartoons, so seminal I probably don't even grasp the extent myself. Comic books: '70's Marvel, Steranko, Starlin, Kane, Kirby, Kirby, Kirby. Steve Gerber, too, but really the artists more than the writers—the possibilities implicit in the art, which the stories themselves were always battening down.

Then R. Crumb, hugely. There are more recent loves, like Dan Clowes and Chester Brown, but that's not influence, not the way you mean. Music, too much to list. Dylan and James Brown and everyone else. Anyway, how does the music influence my narrative art? Probably no good way, not directly. It only keeps me alive and working and thrilled at the fact of expressiveness.

And then painting, the whole idea of painting, which was the 'artistic paradigm' I grew up inside, because of my father's career. I was a painter until I was twenty. The totality more than any one artist. But especially Georgione, Breugel, Ernst, De Chirico, Rothko, Guston, Samaras, Oldenberg, and my father.

PR: If you were to make a list of your books in terms of how successful you were in completing what you set out to do, what would that list look like?
JL: *Girl In Landscape* is the one that's just right and all mine. I can't really look at the books before that, not closely. I suspect *Gun* is a righteous device, ticking along nicely, and *Amnesia Moon* a homely animal I loved too much and abandoned. *As She Climbed*—cute. Then in *Motherless Brooklyn* I maybe put it all together—but that stands outside myself, so I just feel grateful to have been involved. It sort of fell on my head. It's the only one which doesn't need me, never did. It would have found someone to write it, by necessity.

PR: Some writers, younger writers in particular, have the dream of moving to New York as part of their maturation as a writer. What's your view on the advantages/disadvantages of being a writer living in New York?
JL: I'm helpless on this, because growing up in Brooklyn I was too close and still as far away as you can be. As a kid I once tailed Norman Mailer down Montague Street. And once went to a store in Manhattan and had Anthony Burgess sign a book. Otherwise I could have been in Indiana. I threw over the (remotely possible) advantage of access when I dropped out of college and fled to California, just as I threw over the chance of help at college by dropping out, and then never going to grad school. By the time I returned to New York I'd published four books. I can't speak for maturation, but I had the books. Now I enjoy the parties, except when I don't. Not a clue how I'd have dealt with them as an aspiring writer hoping for a break—likely that would have been torment. I was better off oblivious in my garret.

PR: What were some of the practical realities of your early life as a writer? It's a rare exception that a writer has the act of writing as his or her only daily responsibility. What was daily life like for you then, and what is it like now that you have had success?
JL: I worked in bookstores. That's the only job I've held outside this authoring business. I was lucky in that, because the people I worked with all understood what I was doing and didn't hold it against me. I was allowed to keep my health insurance even after I began slimming down my hours, working four days a week, then three, then two. That's unusual. And books were cheap. I worked a combination of dayshifts and nightshifts, and so learned to write at different hours, any hours I could find.

Every moment's stolen.

Now? I write these words from the backseat of a solid milk-chocolate Cadillac, which somehow says it all.

**PR:** What sort of cautionary advice would you give to young writers?

**JL:** Never put a fountain pen in your shirt pocket—that's just asking for it. And don't bother the older writers while they're thinking, or appear to be. ✧

# WHAT DO THE WINNERS OF

THE 2001 PEN/NORA MAGID AWARD FOR
LITERARY EDITING[1]

THE PULITZER PRIZE[2]

THE NATIONAL BOOK AWARD[3]

THE PEN/FAULKNER AWARD[3]

THE PEN/HEMINGWAY AWARD[2]

THE NEW YORK PRIZE FOR BEST DEBUT BOOK[2]

INCLUSION IN THE BEST AMERICAN SHORT
STORIES OF 1999, 2000, AND 2002[2,4]

INCLUSION IN THE BEST AMERICAN POETRY
OF 2001 AND 2002[5]

## HAVE IN COMMON?

## COULD IT BE AGNI?

# THE BEATRICE HAWLEY AWARD

FORREST HAMER

*CALL AND RESPONSE*

MARY SZYBIST

*GRANTED*

B.H. FAIRCHILD

*THE ART OF THE LATHE*

Open to poets nationwide, the winner receives $2000 and publication. Submissions must be postmarked by December 1st, 2002.

# THE NEW ENGLAND / NEW YORK AWARD

MATTHEA HARVEY

*PITY THE BATHTUB ITS FORCED EMBRACE OF THE HUMAN FORM*

TOM THOMPSON

*LIVE FEED*

ALESSANDRA LYNCH

*SAILS THE WIND LEFT BEHIND*

Winners receive $2000, publication, and a one-month residency at the Vermont Studio Center. Writers must live in New England or New York. Submissions must be postmarked by October 1st, 2002.

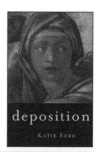

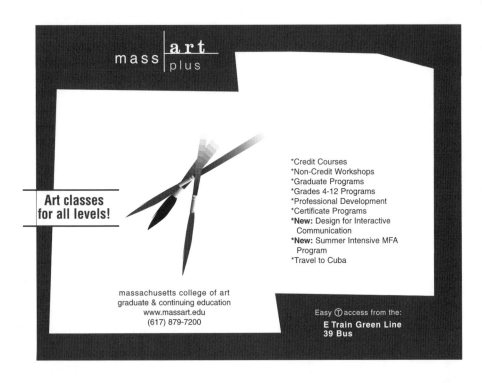

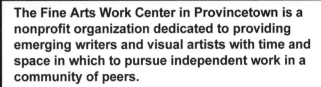

# NOON

NOON

1369 MADISON AVENUE  PMB 298  NEW YORK  NEW YORK  10128-0711

SUBSCRIPTION $9 DOMESTIC AND $14 FOREIGN

# THE MISSOURI REVIEW

Twelfth Annual
## Editors' Prize in Fiction and Essay
and the Sixth Annual
## Larry Levis Editors' Prize in Poetry

## $2000 Fiction | $2000 Essay | $2000 Poetry
Largest prize amounts ever! For a history of our contest
visit our website at www.moreview.org

## Complete Guidelines
(no other information is needed to enter)

Page restrictions: 25 typed, double-spaced, for fiction and nonfiction. Poetry entries can include any number of poems up to 10 pages. Each story, essay, or group of poems constitutes one entry.

Entry fee: $15 for each entry (checks made payable to *The Missouri Review*). Each fee entitles entrant to a one-year subscription to *TMR*, an extension of a current subscription, or a gift subscription (a $7 savings from the regular subscription price). Please indicate your choice and enclose a complete address for subscriptions. Entries must be clearly addressed to:

*Missouri Review* **Editors' Prize**
**1507 Hillcrest Hall, UMC**
**Columbia, MO 65211**

Outside of the envelope must be marked "Fiction," "Essay," or "Poetry." Each entry in each category must be mailed in a separate envelope. Enclose an index card with author's name, address, and telephone number in the left corner and the work's title in the center of the card if fiction or essay. This information should also be included in the first page of the submission.

Entries must be previously unpublished and will not be returned. Enclose #10 SASE or email address for announcement of winners only. In addition to the winners, three finalists in each category will receive awards and be considered for publication.

**Deadline: Entries must be postmarked by 15 October 2002.**

# Listerine: The Life and Opinions of Laurence Sterne

John Wesley Harding

Laurence Sterne was an eighteenth century rock star. His career path was the blueprint for any indie band today. In his home town, far away from the commercial center of the industry, he pressed his first release himself; then, after he had hyped it relentlessly, liberally quoting phoney good reviews, he managed to sell it to a major label honcho, Dodsley, who had built his reputation on acts like classic rocker Pope and straight-edge Stafford revivalist Johnson. Then Sterne went on tour to London, did a bunch of in-stores where he appeared in character. He slept around. He went on a successful European Tour. Before the public tired of his first incarnation, he had smoothly segued into another; he kept them guessing ever after. He courted controversy wherever he could and refused to delineate between himself and his fictional alter egos, allowing truth and lies to mingle. He made a lot of money and died, alone and practically broke. His corpse was stolen from its grave.

I am a man of fancies. I collect Powell and Pressburger memorabilia. I hoard old books of ballads. I am sadly attached to an English football team, Arsenal. I own too many Bob Dylan CDs and books, though nowadays I rarely supplement the collection. But Laurence Sterne is my hobby-horse.

"So long as a man rides his Hobby-Horse peaceably and quietly along the King's High-way, and neither compels you or me to get up behind him.–pray, Sir, what have either you or I to do with it?" But I have agreed to write this essay and therefore that has to change. So here's a crop, here's the stirrup, and Here Comes The Groom.

*The Life And Opinions Of Tristram Shandy, Gentleman* was published serially, in nine volumes, between 1760 and 1767. It caused a huge scandal and was a great success. The book begins, famously, as the narrator tells the story of his own conception. I shan't spoil it for you, but, at the crucial moment, his father is interrupted...

Hold on. Before I get on with this, let me say in my own defence, for I hear the scholars carping already, that a lot of my reference materials—an entire shelf full of Sterne books, not to mention every regional ballad book, my entire vinyl collection &c—are the victims of a recent move to Brooklyn, and therefore *not to hand.* I brought the best and most valuable items with me, naturally, but I am hoping that the others are in a locker in a self-storage facility in Seattle, exactly where I left them. Of course, they could be for sale on a rug on the side of a rainy street. Alternatively, they could be where I left them, but underwater. Storage lockers, I shudder! Nothing can make a person feel less permanent.

Philosophers and psychologists agree. Almost as much has been said about storage lockers as about the mind itself—and isn't the mind, in fact, a kind of storage locker housing, at a cost, memories to which the owner wished he had better access? When you require a particular item, who's to say that it isn't buried under many other items you don't need, obscured from view? Or that you haven't lost the key (or forgotten the access code—for storage lockers move with the times) so long ago did you store it away? And that reminds me that I don't even remember when I first read *Tristram Shandy*.

My father might have been partly responsible. He gave me an antique edition of *A Sentimental Journey*, Sterne's other "novel." When? We can't quite remember but it was some time ago. Why? Perhaps it was something to do with Cambridge.[1] He remembers that he bought it at Lewis & Harris in Trim Street, Bath, which is as good a name for a street as any, as any Sterne fancier will tell you.[2]

There is more to be said about self-storage, and I shall say it shortly, but I have quite forgotten my books, which are still locked up in a self-storage facility in Washington.[3] The inconvenience of this filing system is the reason that I might botch a quote here and there (since memory, on which I must rely, is itself little better than a storage locker as we have seen) or even steal entirely from someone else's work and forget to credit them—if I do, however, remember that Sterne did it first and often. And when he attacked plagiarism in literature, of which he himself had been accused, he plagiarized his comments entirely from Burton's *The*

---

[1] *Laurence Sterne and I have very little in common. However, we both went to Jesus College, Cambridge—coincidentally, exactly 250 years apart.*

[2] *Trim is Uncle Toby's manservant. And while we're about it: Walter Shandy is Tristram's pedantic and hobby-horsical father; Uncle Toby, his sympathetic war veteran uncle, now left impotently playing with toy soldiers in the back garden as he tries to understand how he received his groin injury; Widow Wadman, the woman who thinks she might be able to seduce him. Incidentally, I looked up Lewis & Harris on the internet to see if they still existed but couldn't find them, although I did find out that Lewis and Harris is the largest and northernmost island of the Outer Hebrides in Scotland.*

[3] *Self-Storage is, technically, the term applied to facilities that offer do-it-yourself, month-to-month storage space rental. They are also sometimes referred to as "Mini Storage," or, incorrectly as "Mini Warehouses." Self-Storage differs greatly from warehousing because it is a landlord/tenant relationship. Forty-five states have established laws defining this relationship (though I don't know about the other five.) If anyone is interested in learning more about Self-Storage, then I recommend The "Self-Storage Handbook," published by Jerkov, Inc. It is the only statistical abstract of the Self-Storage Industry. In its pages, you'll find many tables with information about saturation levels, occupancy rates, population and income trends, and more. You'll also find a number of pro forma financial statements.*

*Anatomy Of Melancholy*. So forgive the odd mistake, why don't you? I could have got the books I needed out of the library, I suppose, but I've had a lot of work on. I'm a musician, not an essayist, dear sir. I have:

Songs to write
Samples to steal
Guitars to string
Loops to copy
Lyrics to edit
Recordings to mix
Demos to hear

I could be taking drugs or getting head from a groupie, but instead I have decided to do the most rock'n'roll thing of all and write an essay on Laurence Sterne, while I am making plans for my next album, the working title of which is *The Man With No Shadow*. You will be able to buy this from my web site (www.wesweb.net, which now takes credit cards) not to mention from any record store that deserves the name.

The above is not merely flagrant self-promotion by the way, but also a heartfelt tribute to Laurence Sterne's flagrant self-promotion. Like mine, Sterne's self-promotion brazenly extends into the actual text. The purpose of some of the most notable interruptions to *Tristram Shandy*, and it is a novel of interruptions rather than plot, seems to be solely to promote other works that Sterne, always sensitive to public reaction and a master of self-marketing, was ready to put on sale.

The first of the major interruptions is a sermon, read by Corporal Trim. The sermon is written by Parson Yorick, Sterne's fictional alter ego, and only turns up at all because it falls out of Uncle Toby's copy of the works of Stevinus, the engineer, when Trim gives the book a shake ("letting the leaves fall down, as he bent the covers back..."), much as Yorick's sermon itself is unattached to, and falls out of the book *Tristram Shandy*. It was, of course, a sermon that Sterne had preached himself a few years earlier. "I can not conceive how it is possible...for such a thing as a sermon to have got into my Stevinus," says Uncle Toby. And well might he not understand, when it is in there for reasons entirely outside his world. (I can't take the time right now to explain these characters in depth—I think you should go off and read the novel first. I'll be here when you get back. It will take about a week if you read the notes with care too.)

Trim reads the sermon at great length (how long were you away? I feel that I could have created an entire universe!), and then Tristram, the narrator, declares: "In case the character of Parson Yorick and this sample of his sermons is liked, –that there are now in the possession of the Shandy family, as many as will make a handsome volume, at the world's service, – and much good may they do it."

The ploy worked. Sterne's *Sermons Of Yorick* came out in seven volumes over the next nine years, and the first volume had a list of 650 subscribers, a roll call of the contemporary legislators of taste. The sermons may even have been more popular than *Tristram Shandy*. (I should have figures to hand. We'll leave it at that.)

Other works, however, which Sterne had in mind as possible spin-offs from the text of *Tristram Shandy*, never surfaced. He tries the hard sell on *Slawkenbergius's Tales* (one of which is the long and silliest digression in the book): "If this specimen...and the exquisiteness of his moral should please the world–translated shall a couple of volumes be." But Shandy's translation never made it to publication. Nor did Walter Shandy's *Tristrapaedia* ["you shall read the chapter at your leisure, (if you chuse it) as soon as ever the Tristrapaedia is published"] or his *Life Of Socrates*, or even Sterne's own audacious plans to turn his novel into a play, as a vehicle for none other than the most famous actor of the age:

> O Garrick! What a rich scene of this would thy exquisite powers make! And how gladly would I write such another to avail myself of thy immortality, and secure my own behind it.

I have tried this trick myself. This is from a new song called *For An Actress*:

> So thank me when you're holding your oscar
> I'll never sell your story to the press
> Though sometimes when I'm feeling broke and hopeless
> I'm tempted by the money, I'll confess
> And I wish you very well with your career
> Just as I wished you very well in bed
> And if you ever need some soundtrack music
> I write that shit standing on my head.

It has had limited success for me, thus far. Worked like a charm for Sterne however.

Fifteen minutes ago, or that's how long it seems,[4] I promised you some more thoughts on storage lockers. But for now let me quote this:

> Employ yourself in improving yourself
> by other men's writings,

---

[4] *I admit that I wrote the section you have just read later than the bit you're reading now, and have subsequently repositioned it by the genius of editing—and you can tell it was my own genius because otherwise I wouldn't have known a single thing about it.*

so that you shall gain easily
what others have laboured hard for.
*—Socrates*

This is taken from the most recent copy of The Self-Storage Association Newsletter, in the Off The Shelf section of "News and Views."[5] Walter Shandy, that devoted collector of trivia, would have agreed.

*The Life And Opinions Of Tristram Shandy, Gentleman* was published serially, in nine volumes, between 1760 and 1767. It caused a huge scandal and was a great success. It did many things that novels hadn't done before, and a few things that none have bothered to do since. Its author, Laurence Sterne, was a congenitally sickly curate. The first pair of volumes was published when he was 46 years old. The book is full of many typographical eccentricities.

**An Itemised List:**

Marbled Page (III, xxxvi – "motly emblem of my work")
Black Page (I, xii – mourns the death of Yorick)
Empty Chapters (IX, xviii, xix)
Blank Page (VI, xxxviii)
Ten Missing Pages, Torn Out Chapter (IV, xxiv)
Official Beginning of Book (IV, xxxii)
Chapter ends in a comma (II, xiv)
Major Interruptions (e.g. The Sermon – II, xvii, Ernulfus' Curse—III, xi; and Slawkenbergius's Tale – (IV, i.)
Amusing Squiggles (VI, xl; IX, iv)
Advice to skip a chapter (I, iv)
The sale of the dedication to the book (I, ix)

These bits of Pre-Postmodernism are built on the foundation of a very strong and sympathetically observed group of characters (the members of the Shandy family and the people who have dealings with them). It is these two opposing facets of the book that have kept it alive and admired for so long. Put simply, in the 19th century, the content ensured the fame of the book, and in the 20th, it was the form.

In the 21st century, you can go on eBay and find a single by a rock group from 1973 called Tristram Shandy. They are a hairy looking bunch, and I didn't buy it despite the fact that the b-side was called "Hunky Funky Woman," perhaps a sly reference to the Widow Wadman. However, the fact that the band existed was recorded in the notable "Annual Volume devoted to Laurence Sterne and His Works," *The Shandean Vol 11* (p.152), and I felt it counted as my first important (and unattributed, but there's a

---

[5] *I have to get on with this essay, but for further storage locker wisdom, I'd like to send you to: http://www.selfstorage.org , the homepage of The Self Storage Association.*

certain dignity in that) contribution to Sterne studies.

Though I wouldn't meet the $10 reserve for this single, this morning on eBay, I bid successfully for the first continental version of "Yorick's Letters To Eliza." Published in 1776, these are Sterne's love letters to the object of his obsessive sentimental affection Eliza Draper, who was sailing home to India and her husband. He was never to see her again. The lister of the item had called the lot "Rare Letters From Yorick to Eliza 1776" and described it as "Written in Olde English this book is in good condition for its age. Part 2 Sternes (sic) Letters to his friends on various occasions to which is added his history of a watch coat." Sterne's name, spelled correctly, appeared nowhere in the listing—these grammatical computer searches are punctilious. Therefore, very few people saw the book, unless, like me, they were searching, with hobby-horsical thoroughness, for "Yorick"—which generally finds you nothing more than a "Yorick Like Skull—VERY REAL."

By the way, I note that you can now look up my email address on eBay. To save you the effort, I shall give it to you right here: jwh@armory.com. Your mail can sit in my inbox, perchance to be included in *The Publick's Letters to JWH,* right alongside letters from the teenage girl who has some pictures to show me, the person who thinks I need some new printer ink cartridges, the man who thinks I have so much trouble with debt that I want to create a new credit profile, and, my most regular unanswered correspondent, the woman who thinks that my penis is too small.

I will put my newly acquired *Journal To Eliza* (by any other name) between my Italian first edition of *Tristram Shandy,* all 11 volumes of *The Shandean* (1989-2000), the 1775 copy of *Letters From Yorick To Eliza* (one of the most beautiful books I've ever seen) and, best of all, my nine volume first edition of *Tristram Shandy.*

As you know, this means that in a small study in my well-appointed apartment somewhere in Brooklyn—I can't be too specific for obvious reasons—I can look at Laurence Sterne's actual handwriting whenever I want. What? You didn't know that? Then I suggest that you go back and read the last paragraph again. I clearly stated that I had Sterne's handwriting here. You didn't notice? I thought that any informed reader would probably know that *any true first edition of Tristram Shandy is signed by Sterne in Vols. V, VII, and IX.* The first four volumes had been so successful and had spawned so many bootlegs and imitations that by Vol. V, Sterne took the unlikely step of sitting at the printers and signing every single copy.[6] Like my last record, *The Confessions Of St. Ace,* an unsigned copy is rarer than a signed one.

---

[6] *On the first pages of Chapters One of Vols V and VII: "L.Sterne." He had more ink in VII but gave the "t" a larger flourish in V. My Vol IX is, unusually, signature free.*

Once you have a man's signature once, do you really need it again, let alone a third time? If you are an autograph collector, you do.[7] I received this letter not two minutes ago via my fan club account. It pinged before me and was hard to ignore, so timely were its contents:

We are two of your biggest fans. Can you please send us two autographed photos, one for each of us? It would mean so much to us if we can have the autograph of our true hero, idol, role model, and inspiration. We will cherish the autograph because we know it will be from our favourite person in the world! Thanks for your time and we hope to me [sic] you live some day.

They want to me me? This one I received yesterday:

Mr Harding - Hello. So wonderful to finally make contact with you. I wanted to drop you a note to let you know how much I have admired you for quite some time. I think the work you do is fantastic and the world would be better off with more positive roles models such as yourself. I hear that some famous people often send their fans signed photographs and I was wondering if you'd be kind enough to send me one. I realise that being a huge celebrity is bound to keep you busy but I'm not looking for anything special. Just your signature without any inscription on a photograph would be fine. I would be very thankful if you would send the photo to me at.

The faux naivety of "I hear that some famous people often send their fans..."! And the "yes, this item is going straight to eBay" charm of "Just your signature without any inscription on a photograph would be fine!" And what is this "role model" nonsense?

One weekend about a year ago, I received about twenty emails, all of which had a similarly peculiar tone—an unctuous tone better suited to a letter to a TV star than little old me, sitting here in my towelling dressing gown thinking about doing the washing up. It was as if they'd all been written by the same person, and that that person had never really heard any of my music. They were generic, full of how long the writer had been trying to get in touch with me—and any fool can get in touch with me just by going to my web site, or, now, reading this essay. So, I began politely asking people where they had got my email address. One honest soul in Florida told me, frankly, that my name had been added to the list of "successful new addresses" at Stararchive.com with a note next to it that said

---

[7] *Autographs are fascinating. Autograph hounds even more so. The autograph says: I am a celebrity and I once wrote my name on this piece of paper that you are now looking at. I have signed this piece of paper to authenticate the fact that I have signed this piece of paper. My hand was here. I admit to owning a few autographs myself, some even outside the covers of books: Noddy Holder of Slade (the first autograph I ever got), James Brown ('It's a Man's World!'), David Seaman ('Safe Hands'), Cliff Richard, J.D.Salinger, Rin Tin Tin (pawprint)...*

something along the lines of "address tested, free signed photo sent within in three days." (Translation: "Take advantage of this sucker whether you've heard of him or not!") And YES, there I am on their web site, between Ty Hardin and Tonya Harding (not somewhere you'd want to be under ANY circumstances). Here is my "address history" as reported by Stararchive.com:

Type: Success
Sent: 1/1/1999, Rcvd: 5/1/2000
Tester's comment: "Talk about diligent! A few days after I e-mailed Wes, he hand-wrote me a letter from San Francisco saying that he'd get right on it. About six months later, he sent me a postcard from Paris, apologising for the delay, but explaining that he was waiting for new PR photos. Almost a year later, he finally sent me a very nice personally inscribed 8x10!"

This might have been a bona fide fan, for even I, in my friendliness, wouldn't bother to send a postcard from Paris, unless I thought the person really wanted my autograph pretty badly. And what do you get for being thoughtful?

Type: Success
Sent: 2/28/2000, Rcvd: 3/16/2000
Tester's comment: "received 8x10 colour performance still, signed."

By this time, I now note from my report card, I had wised up. The next entry is a disappointed and rather terse:

Type: Success
Sent: 3/13/2001, Rcvd: 3/14/2001
Tester's comment: "Must send via postal mail."

Now the comment by my name reads:

"For an autograph, a SASE must be sent to this address. No autographs will be sent out from an email approach."

Here's one really good one before I get back to the body of this essay, which I feel I have been unfairly ignoring. (However, the essay has progressed in my absence. Autographs will turn out to have much to do with the subject itself, and the wheels of scholarship have not been spinning but turning all along. We are involved in something, like *Tristram Shandy*, both digressive and progressive.) But I would be unfair not to let you read this one:

Dear Mr. Harding, I just wanted to send you this quick note to tell you I admire your impervious dedication and tremendous strive that you display in the spotlight. I'm not only a big fan, but I appreciate the work you put in and the success you have encountered. Keep up the good work. Would it be possible for you to send an autograph? I appreciate the time you have taken to read this E-mail. Have a good day.

The last time I asked for somebody's autograph was when I was staying at Shandy Hall, Sterne's vicarage in Coxwold, Yorkshire. It is now owned by the Laurence Sterne Trust and houses the most incredible collection of Sterneiana. In the lovely gardens, there is a converted building, Wolfson Cottage, where you can stay. Yes, *you* can actually stay there. I actually stayed there during the 1998 World Cup.[8] I was on holiday with a woman—no, I am not married—she might have been my sister! My mother!—anyway, it's the 21st century when a man can holiday with whom he chooses or who chooses him—and we walked along the valley, past the ruins of Byland Abbey (where Sterne said he saw Cordelia's Grave) and ate some tremendous pub food (which included Black Pudding with Ginger Crème Fraiche, and they weren't serving that in 1760). "I'm as happy as a prince in this rich valley underneath the Hambleton Hills," wrote Sterne in 17something-or-other, let's say 55. I could check this fact, but I'm writing in such a hurry, that I have no time to recollect or look. I remember that we were having such a Shandean time of it while we were there, that Shelley Jackson (for it was she! Coincidentally, the author of *The Melancholy Of Anatomy*, released in April 2002 by Anchor Books) saw a bottle of Listerine by the bedside and misread it as a bottle of "L. Sterne," which it is if you blur your i's.

In Shandy Hall, I was able to sit for some time, and entirely unmonitored, in what was (and still is) Sterne's study. Guided tours go round once or twice a week, but sightseers are only allowed to peer into the study. I was surrounded by many first editions of all Sterne's books, all signed, doubtless in volume IX too.[9] I was surrounded by thousands of his autographs and even loose versions of his signature cut from title pages, tipped out (it's the opposite of "tipped in") of various copies of *Tristram Shandy*, which now, because of some antique dealer's GREED and STUPIDITY, have a small signature-sized piece of paper cut out of the title page.

That day, I made a cold phone call, from a cold phone booth, and visited the house of Nic Jones, legendary English folk musician. Nic Jones

---

[8] *I am informed that the Sterne tourist trade might be down because of people's UNFOUNDED fear of Foot and Mouth disease. Tourists all! Go to Shandy Hall! Don't be put off by Word of Foot and Mouth!*

[9] *See footnote vi.*

had a car crash in 1981 and has been recovering ever since. Of the five albums he made before his accident, four are entirely unavailable, due to the GREED and STUPIDITY of the man who now, supposedly, owns the copyright. I hadn't even *seen* a copy of his first album *Ballads and Songs.* On that visit, Nic gave me one, and, of course, I asked him to sign it. (I admired his "impervious dedication and tremendous strive," so what else could I do?) Later on that year, in Seattle, I made *Trad Arr Jones,* an album of my versions of Nic Jones' arrangements of folk songs.

If that idea pleases the publick, they (you) can buy that album for $15 from my web page (www.wesweb.net), which still takes credit cards. And if that *anecdote* pleases the publick, then I will shortly make available a small collection of my anecdotes in a thin volume published by Small Beer Press entitled *Anecdotes of John Wesley Harding*—it's hardly going to win the Booker Prize, though it would be nice to be nominated. Ah, but I was talking about Sterne's self-promotion.


Making *Tristram Shandy* an overnight sensation took some time. Ten months earlier, Sterne had been refused by a London publisher as too great a risk, so he had the first two volumes printed in York (the true first edition) at his own cost, with the London publisher's assistance. Copies in hand, Sterne then dictated a letter to his mistress, who signed it as her own words and sent it to her influential friend, Garrick ("There are two volumes just published here, which have made a great noise, and have had a prodigious run...it has a great character as a witty smart book.") Sterne sent copies to Garrick, who was at the height of his fame, and the book began to make its way in London. By the time Sterne arrived in the Capital, the copies he had sent ahead were entirely sold out, and Dodsley, the publisher, made him an offer for a new edition and the next two volumes. Sterne was a star. He had gone straight to number one.

If Sterne's overnight fame had happened today:

• *Shandy-O-Poly* ("Oh, I've landed on Shandy Hall again!" RENT!)
• *The Life And Opinions Of Harry Potter, Schoolboy* (a masterpiece of cross-marketing)
• "Uncle Toby" series Toy Soldiers (pewter, sold through Skymall magazines)
• Monogrammed Yorick dog collar
• Free collectable plastic "character statuettes" with every Kid's McMeal
• CD of songs "inspired by" the book *Tristram Shandy*
• Pokeshan trading cards
• Laurence Sterne on Howard Stern ('C'mon, Larry, the sentimental stuff is just a cover for the real action, right?")

As it was, the book was so successful that it gave its name to a card game, a soup, and a dance. There were bootleg editions of existing volumes, spurious editions of future volumes that Sterne had yet to write, and responses to the book in the form of parodies, "admonitory lyric epistles," and out and out put-downs of Sterne and his work. But in 1760, there was no higher proof of real fame than to be the subject of a broadside ballad, and there was more than one written about *Tristram Shandy*. I wish Nic Jones had recorded one so I could have put it on *Trad Arr Jones*, but he didn't, so it will be up to me to revive these forgotten masterpieces. Here's a verse of the ballad "Tristram Shandy":

> He tells you too ma'am in the act of coition
> His mother had chanced all the sport to have spoiled
> For she interrupted the midst of fruition
> With questions none would have asked but a child
> Just when his strong motion
> Was pouring the lotion
> That would all the sorrows of life have beguiled
> She asked him a question so odd
> And said while she tickled his codd
> My dear have you wound up the clock.

It shows a fairly close reading of the text.[10]

It wasn't just the book, but Sterne himself that was a sensation. And he did his utmost to confuse himself with his creation. For 46 years, Sterne had staked his hopes on kindness at the hands of others, in his placement at college or in his preferments in the church. But with *Tristram Shandy* he took his future into his own hands. Robert Zimmerman became Bob Dylan, and perhaps even has trouble remembering who Robert Zimmerman was. So Laurence Sterne became Yorick and Shandy. He understood that, having staked the book on his own character, he was as much the subject as the Shandy family, and he was there-

---

[10] *Oh, another verse, if you insist. That was the third and this is the sixth:*

*Then when your husband lies over your belly, ma'am*
*Take special care and mind what you're about*
*Or else you may stop up his river of jelly, ma'am*
*How then shall the homunculus paddle out*
*O humour his motion*
*And suck in the potion*
*His mettlesome squirt shall whitewash you each bout*
*And when he in amorous Pinn*
*At love's door gives the conjugal knock*
*Rise up and at once let him in*
*    Nor think about winding the clock.*

fore prepared to enter London society in whichever guise he thought best suited the occasion, sometimes the bawdy Tristram, or sometimes the kindly, sentimental country parson. He was a walking commercial for his own novels and "Shandied it" through London Society. In a letter to his girlfriend of the time, he mentions Reynolds' portrait of him and adds: "so I shall make the most of myself, & sell both inside & out." Unlike other contemporary novelists who liked to opine in their own character for a chapter here and there before returning to the labyrinthine plot, Sterne made his own character the entire novel; he made himself, and his thoughts, the star. As if to say: "I am the novel. Read me."

Sterne understood the demands of the marketplace, and in an age where Gray still thought it more dignified to sign over his own royalties to his publisher and a few years before Swift had declined, as a Dean, to profit from his own works, Sterne was ready to bargain with his publishers and make large show of his profits. He had sold two volumes of his sermons before the third volume of Shandy was released—he had just happened to bring them to London with him. He actively intrigued for Hogarth (it had worked with Garrick, after all), the greatest artist of the day, to do engravings for the second edition of Volume I (in which he was entirely successful, for both the artist and the writer had a keen eye for commerce) at a time when very few contemporary novels were illustrated. He finally dedicated the book to less significant a figure than Pitt, the Prime Minister. His ambitions were huge and his marketing strategies, I can't think of a better term for them, clever and new. He would have been all over the internet. He'd have been writing his own reviews on Amazon before the book even came out.

Sterne played with identity in a very modern way—in the character of Yorick, he charmed women with sentiment; in the character of Shandy, he shocked Samuel Johnson by showing him an indecent picture at a dinner; in the guise of a young woman, he hyped his own success. He encouraged people to muddle Sterne the vicar with Yorick the parson, Sterne the writer with Shandy the writer—at times in the book he forgets that Shandy isn't a parson, so thin is the line between himself and his character. In an age when arguments about plagiarism and authorship were rife, his "novel" was a compendium of other people's thoughts and writing, mostly uncredited. Sterne wrote two novels but, remarkably, his name appears not once in the collected eleven volumes of both books. *Tristram Shandy* was written by "Shandy" himself and *A Sentimental Journey* was written by "Mr. Yorick." But when it comes time to prove his authorship of the volumes, the signature "L.Sterne" sits in these books and says: I wrote this, not the bootleggers or the parodists or the balladeers, but me, Laurence Sterne. Self-promoted, self-released, Sterne toyed with identity and made the reader wonder, "who is the author?" He was who you wanted him to be. And when the sales dipped, he became someone else.

In case I am making Sterne sound like a chancer, he was. But there are many reasons to love him. As Christopher Ricks says: "Sterne's greatness is not simply that he wrote a novel about writing a novel; his triumph is due to the fact that (unlike most of his imitators) he gave as much genius to his invented world (the characters of Mr. Shandy and Toby) as to the theme of inventing it."[11] He also gave as much genius to the characterization, on and off the page, of the inventor himself, his greatest invention of all. The three things are evenly balanced, and this has assured the novel's relevance from 1767 to me, here, now. The novel has seemed modern in one way or another ever since the day it was written.[12]

This has made it the victim of many a critic's own hobbyhorse. Depending on whom you believe, it is either finished or it is unfinished; it is a Boswellian intimate biography, a "musical novel," "the last classical narrative," either crypto-feminist or mysogynist, a "futuristic poem in an extra-rational language"; it is a direct precursor to Modernism placing Sterne as a prophet and the creator of the stream of consciousness novel, or an early work of Romanticism; it is firmly in the tradition of Learned Wit or an exercise of rhetoric in a Post-Lockean world, and either in the mainstream of the conservative, moralistic, augustan tradition, or the start of the ironic novel. Or it isn't, in fact, a novel at all.[13] Like Sterne, *Tristram Shandy* is whatever the reader wants it to be.


Time and a word count are snapping at our heels. I am going to start an earlier paragraph again from the beginning. I left a point suspendu, but it has been trop suspendu.

*Tristram Shandy* begins, famously, as the narrator tells the story of his own conception. Again, I shan't spoil it for you, but, at the crucial moment

---

[11] *Christopher Ricks' excellent introduction to the Penguin Classic edition of* Tristram Shandy.

[12] *The 18th century ecclesiastic Archdeacon William Paley, when asked what his three favorite things in life were, answered: "Baked potatoes in their jackets, blowing hot air into your shoes with a pair of bellows in winter, and reading* Tristram Shandy.*"*

[13] *And did Sterne even think it was a novel? He quotes and cites Burton and Montaigne but never Fielding, Richardson or Smollett. It is definitively time for me to say something original, in a critical vein, about* Tristram Shandy. *However, fearing that I will be unable to do so, I have decided to quote someone else saying something original. It happens to be one of my favorite bits of Shandean criticism. Jeffrey Williams' "Narrative of Narrative (* Tristram Shandy*)" published in MLN 105 (1990): 1032-45: "*Tristram Shandy *is a narrative of narrative. The so-called narrative intrusions and comments actually form a linear narrative whose subject is the composing of a narrative." "This sequence could then be given: E (C (Ca, A, Aa)- C (A, B)- C (A, B)- C (B, Cd)- Cs- C (Cs, A, B)- D (Dd)- B- B). The plot(s) could be reductively summarized: E (C-C-C-C-Cs-C-D-B-B), factoring out the level of narration. From these notations, we should be able to see that the overall shape of the novel is fairly simple."*

of his conception, his father is interrupted by his mother with dire results. (One of the charming things about the book is that it is almost impossible to explain what happens in it.) Tristram is doomed from birth due to this screwed-up insemination. The "homunculus," the fully formed miniature human that the eighteenth-century "animunculists" believed was found in sperm, is dispersed haphazardly on his path to "the place destined for his reception," rather than being escorted in safety by his father's animal spirits.

> What if any accident had befallen him in his way alone?—or that, thro terror of it, natural to so young a traveller, my little gentleman had got to his journey's end miserably spent:– his muscular strength and virility worn down to a thread;....and that in this sad disorder'd state of nerves, he had laid down a prey to sudden starts, or a series of melancholy dreams and fancies for nine long, long months together.

It is also the book itself that is being shot haphazardly into the world, at the hands of a writer who is very much unlike Fielding's prescient all-seeing, all-knowing narrator. Sterne, in the guise of Shandy, doesn't know quite where to begin the story of his life and keeps on interrupting himself, and his own animal spirits, as the book repeatedly fails to get going. He doesn't know where to start, or how to continue. A few pages later, Shandy confirms that he was born on 5th November 1718 and:

> That in every stage of my life, and at every turn and corner where she could get fairly at me, the ungracious Duchess has pelted me with a set of as pitiful misadventures and cross accidents as ever small hero sustained.

The homunculus is the "little gentleman," and Shandy is the "small hero"—both entering the world, doomed by their authors. Immediately the narrative enlists a literal, and figurative, midwife. After conception, small hero and novel must be born.


Sterne's breadth of useless knowledge is quite fantastic. Learned, punctilious, and arcane discourses litter the book. There is a moment in Tom Stoppard's most recent play, *The Invention of Love*, which I can't find in the script that I bought ($12 that I spent especially so I could quote it accurately to you people, demanding audience that you are) where A. E. Housman says to someone or someone says to him that, though useless knowledge is the most important kind of knowledge (and you may have noticed that I am paraphrasing), useful knowledge is good too, though for the faint-hearted.

Although he makes mock as he revels in the trivia and the absurd paradoxes, nothing is too obscure to merit consideration for Sterne (or Walter Shandy). The book is a huge compendium of quack belief and, at times, a freak show of human oddities past and present. (Wonder at the glass people who live on Mercury! Marvel at the baby who can speak Latin at the age of four months!) It also functions as a knowing satire on contemporary characters and issues: the argument "Midwife vs. Male Doctor" takes up whole chapters. Whether a child may be baptized before birth is another knotty issue, the excuse for a lengthy dinner conversation (during which a male character gets a hot chestnut dropped down his trousers). The Doctors of the Sorbonne, it turns out, have decreed that baptism can be administered before the baby is born, by injection into the mother: "par le moyen d'une petite canaille.–Anglice, a squirt." And the chapter concludes that perhaps it can be done *after* marriage, but *before* the child is even conceived (think about this carefully) "par le moyen d'une petite canulle, and, sans faire aucun tort a le pere." I can't translate that, as it makes me wince.

The small gentlemanly heroes (Tristram/Homunculus) are both brought into life by a different squirt (the doomed squirt). "Are children bought into the world with a squirt?" Toby asks at one point, and a few pages later, Shandy/Sterne refers to the "rash jerks, and hare-brained squirts" of his pen... "spurting (his) ink" over his tables and his books. The Pen is, one might say, mightier than the penis, but they both spew forth unexpectedly.[14]

Such double meanings pervade *Tristram Shandy*. Sterne can hold two focuses at once—one finds oneself in the middle of a metaphor that turns out to be the subject, or a completely new subject that, with the deft turn of a corner, becomes a remark on a narrative thread one had entirely forgotten. As in Nabokov's *Pale Fire*[15], there is both a text and a commentary upon the text by a narrator who is not what he claims to be and believes things that may make him technically insane. (Sterne himself was no more insane than Nabokov,[16] although his wife did think she was the Queen Of Bohemia.)

We find the truly Shandean at the meeting place of the arcane and the bawdy. There are long disquisitions on buttonholes and noses, things that he finds it "morally impossible" that the reader should understand. It was

---

[14] *I am thinking of getting a tattoo in the shape depicted in Vol IX, iv. It depicts the flourish of Corporal Trim's stick (which "seems to resemble eighteenth-century illustrations of the motions of a spermatozoon"—from the notes to the Florida edition of* Shandy *written by editors who, appropriately, have chosen it as the cover for all five volumes of the complete Sterne thus far published.)*

[15] *It was only during this reading that I found mention in* Tristram Shandy *of "Nova Zembla." In* Pale Fire, *Zembla is the name of the kingdom of which the professor believes himself to be exiled royalty.*

[16] *The author of* Lolita *was, however, unable to listen to music with pleasure.*

this feigned delicacy that Thackeray found "bad" and "wicked": "There is not a page in Sterne's writing but has something that were better away, a latent corruption—a hint, as of an impure presence." Sterne pretended that he was hiding the bawdiness while actually revelling in it.[17] And the man was a *vicar* for goodness sake!

The seduction of the reader is indeed his prime concern. Yet, right next to this naughtiness can be a moment of genuine delicacy, because, for Sterne, there were no rules. The Shandean tone was not an arch postmodern joke but an act of liberation, or at least, something he was inventing as he went along. This is what Nietzsche and Goethe admired in him. Sterne says, "(I) shall confine myself neither to [Horace's] rules, nor to any man's rules that ever lived."

The Shandean tone was ignored by English Literature for 150 years while it turned to the solid moral certainties of the nineteenth-century novel.[18] After his death, Sterne's unfinished *A Sentimental Journey* (written by Yorick, of course, not by the depraved Shandy) became his pre-eminent work, better suited to the times, and *Tristram Shandy*, with its trickery and wickedness, was put on the back burner, forgotten in favor of the sentiment that would finally find its apotheosis in the death of Little Nell some years later. Today, the sentiment of the unfinished *Journey* seems rather embarrassing, but the truth is that the book is neither entirely sincere and sentimental nor a parody of Sentimentalism (both

---

17 *He teases us with his own indiscretions—because the novel is, after all, all about him. He had staked the novel on his own character and he omitted very little, much in the way that modern art dares you to equate the artist with the person depicted in the art—even his astonishing addiction to seduction and adultery. Perhaps the reader thinks that Jenny, to whom he refers, is his mistress: "Is it not impossible but that my dear, dear Jenny! Tender as the appellation is, may be my child.... Nor is there any thing unnatural or extravagant in the supposition, that my dear Jenny may be my friend.——Friend!— My friend.— Surely, Madam, a friendship between the two sexes may subsist, and be supported without———Fy! Mr. Shandy:—— Without any thing, Madam, but that tender and delicious sentiment, which ever mixes in friendship, where there is a difference of sex."*

18 *And that's a very long 19th century. The 19th century may have lasted until James Joyce wrote to a friend, describing* Finnegan's Wake: *"I am trying to build many planes of narrative within a single aesthetic purpose. Did you ever read Laurence Sterne?" Sometimes the Shandean Tone even pops up in the popular song of today:*

*"I'd love to get inside your head*
*And let's be blunt*
*There are other words*
*That rhyme as well"*

*("Too Much into Nothing" by John Wesley Harding, from* The Confessions Of St.Ace, *Mammoth, 2001. Printed by kind permission of me. As the commentator notes in "Notes Towards A Clarification Of The Confessions Of St.Ace": "(I) can only have my suspicions that one of the words that 'rhyme(s) as well' is bed. Also suggested have been: shed ['I'd like to get inside your shed' is highly believable], homestead, and less likely, Samoyed." But the commentator, Dick Sharpley, might have missed the point entirely—what if the rhyme was "blunt" rather than "bed"?)*

have been claimed). Its style is inclusive and allows one to laugh and to feel, and the tone is entirely, incredibly, ambiguous. The genius is that it can be read both as sincere and as a clever parody of the excesses of such sincerity. Can I even think of anything to compare it to? It is Sterne's ability to pull the audience this way and that that is so astonishing. He was able to invent and destroy at the same time. A modern equivalent might be the tone of the Randy Newman songs where he gets to have his cake and eat it too (or leave his hat on and take it off), like "You Can Leave Your Hat On." His most popular songs are first person character studies of various deviants: racists, rapists, and assorted bigots. This is unusual in rock music, where the audience basically wants the "I" of the song to be the "I" of the singer. I blame the few singers who had both interesting personal lives and were good writers, Bob Dylan included. "Sincerity is the enemy of art"—I think Oscar Wilde said that. Or if he didn't, he should have.

Once I was on a singer-songwriter panel (and please may I not make that mistake too often in the future, unless there's someone I really want to meet on the panel, an autograph I need, as it were) and, after a number of my co-panellists had said how the song they were going to sing was about their girlfriend who beat them up, or a boy they broke up with in high school, I said that I made most of my songs up, that I prioritized the imagination. I sang "Miss Fortune," which is about a boy found in a ditch by a rich man. He is brought up as a girl and inherits a fortune.[19] The first line is:

I was born with a coathanger in my mouth....[20]

I love this song and I love to sing it. At the end of the song, a co-panellist said, rather sneeringly: "Well, that didn't mean anything to you at all, did it?" And that's the problem. It didn't happen to me, but that doesn't mean that it doesn't mean anything to me. And if it had happened to me, would it make it any more interesting?[21] "My Way" didn't *happen* to Sinatra. He didn't even write it, but people believed it when he sang it, and that's show business. (Writing your own song is a comparatively recent thing anyway. Blame Bob Dylan for that too.)

A song doesn't have to pretend not to be a work of artifice to move me, and might move me quite as much if it makes me aware that it is. With regard to books, people are still sometimes suspicious of those

---

[19] *Shortly to become a novel. No, it really is. I added this footnote later and hope it doesn't mess up the numbering of the others. For a very funny tale of misnumbered footnotes, see Jonathan Coe's novel* The House Of Sleep.

[20] *From* Awake, *Appleseed Recordings, 2001*

[21] *I've lost count of the number of times I've died in my songs. It has yet to happen in real life (at time of writing).*

postmodern tricksters who draw attention to the fictionality of the story or the reality of the book that the reader is holding, and look back nostalgically to a past when stories were told more straightforwardly. Yet here at the very dawn of the novel is *Tristram Shandy*, an astonishingly successful book that is entirely self-conscious and playful with regards to its bookishness. I don't think I've ever read a book that makes you quite so aware that you are reading an actual book, literally and physically—it suggests that, if you're weary, you sit down on a pile of them ("do, Sir, sit down upon a set, they are better than nothing"), that if you are bored, you skip a few pages; it defies you to notice that some pages have literally been removed (torn out by the angry author). The typographical eccentricities remind the reader that he is a reader, and that her experience is unique and entirely different from any other reader's experience. In the case of the marbled page, because marbling is not an exact science, every single copy of the book is actually different because no two marblings can be alike. (You can imagine asking a publisher to do this today in the first edition of your first book. "Hey, that's a great idea!" your editor would say to you, "but we have an even better idea—how about we *don't* do it!")

When I sat down, my intention was to write a good essay; and "as far as the tenuity of my understanding would allow, a wise one." But I have run out of time. In *Tristram Shandy* too, time is the enemy. Sterne himself is dogged by the ill health that will eventually kill him, and to which he makes constant reference. Life goes by too quickly for Tristram to write it all down, particularly as he has started by having to go so far backwards: how will he ever catch up? Even his father's *Tristrapaedia*, the book that will educate his son, mirrors this problem. Tristram grows too fast for his father's pen (which "was a little retrograde") to catch up. There is much play on the concept of digression and narrative time: "It is about an hour and a half's tolerable good reading since my Uncle Toby rung the bell...so that no-one can say, with reason, that I have not allowed Obadiah time enough, poetically speaking, and considering the emergency too, both to go and come."[22] Actual dates litter the pages as Sterne writes:

Vol I, xviii – March 9, 1759
Vol I, lxxi – March 26, 1759 (between 9 and 10 in the morning)
Vol V, xvii – August 10, 1761
(This Essay – August 10, 2001, just after noon)
Vol IX, i – August 12, 1766

Death of Sterne: March 18, 1768. *A Sentimental Journey Through*

---

[22] *See Vol II, viii—one of my favorite chapters.*

*France And Italy. By Mr. Yorick* was published three weeks before Sterne's death. When Sterne died, he lifted up his right arm as if defending himself from a blow, and said "Now it is come." His body was dug up and sold for dissection, and it was only when Sterne's face was recognised by students, on a slab at a university, that his remains were returned for reburial. A relative of Mrs. Sterne's went to Sterne's rooms and took charge of his personal effects and papers, most of which he destroyed. His daughter Lydia misedited his letters, inserting her own name instead of Eliza Draper's in some of the sentimental love letters that Sterne wrote to his girlfriend weeks before he died. Even after his death, his identity and his remains continued to shift.

The death of Le Fever in *Tristram Shandy*:

> Nature instantly ebbed again,- the film returned to its place,- the pulse fluttered-stopped-went on-throbbed-stopped again-moved-stopped-shall I go on?-No. ✧

# ART

## POST ROAD

# Takahiro Kimura: Destruction and Construction of the Human Face

Introduction by Chris Elam

The subway doors ease closed, hissing, and then I falter, lurching forward, regaining balance with my eyes. Through the window, its dusty veined surface, I see forms. Rumpled, bent, slack, suspended bodies, followed by passages of darkness, light, and then faces! We're traveling at the same speed, frames per second, as the faces flicker before me. What infinite, abbreviated pleasure, the eyes, noses, chins, beards, earrings, berets, gold teeth, the emotions of an entire day flexed and flattened between tunnel pylons. What a privileged position, the queer and discomforting intimacy. These expressions caught between panes of glass, fissured, emotions elusive, these faces caught between expressions. And then there is just one face, her head bent forward, soft red cap, turtleneck. Her lips are moving, eyes downcast, as a tremor cuts across her cheek. She turns, the merest moment exchanged, eyes half-crazed, looking at me, through me...no, just through the glass, cracked and forlorn. Just as quickly I slow, her lips smear, eyes torn away, gone, to a full stop.

Stooping, I notice a faint white shape in the dirt. Eyeing it closely, taking it up, I discover a figure has been drawn in colored pens on the surface. It's a small square notebook, the round restless face of a young boy sketched on the cover. He looks at me keenly through layers of dust. Turning to the second page, I see again the boy, but now a slight sneer mars his lips. Then another page, and again the boy, this time a budding smirk, his face less round, firmer, unmistakably changed. Turning again, and again, each page reveals a new face, slightly transformed -- surely older. Flipping quickly to the last page reveals the wrinkled shrunken head of an elderly man, eyes shut. With this understanding, I now investigate more closely each life stage. Whether backwards or forwards, facets of his face are revealed, then taken away, and yet they return again, slightly altered, resolute. Layer upon layer of life lived – ever relived as memory. Rain has caused stains, like filigree marbling the boy's face; and certain sheets are missing, having been torn out, the steady advance punctuated, the false starts that texture a life's surface, in every glance ultimately a mirror. A page falls off in my hand, and, hesitating a moment...I push it into my pocket, and then return the little notebook to the ground.

Looking at the faces of Takahiro Kimura, you have the feeling that you're back where you started, looking again, for the second or third time. That in a way you've been beside Takahiro all along, as he's found the photos in magazines, randomly, and then torn their faces into pieces, reconfiguring them before painting the resulting image. For such is your wonder, your sense of sheer discovery, grounded in the deepest familiarity. Not of form necessarily, but of mood, expression and, most importantly, emotion. Takahiro has deconstructed and reconstructed the human face as if with panes of glass, or, more, planes of emotion, applied with the care and resonance of someone looking not at his model...but at you the viewer. Discovering what both you and he – what we all – conceal behind our constructed layers. Thus the undeniable mastery of Takahiro's medium, while rooted in color, line, texture, is equally his deft wielding of the mirror.  ✧

APR 7
2000
No. 44

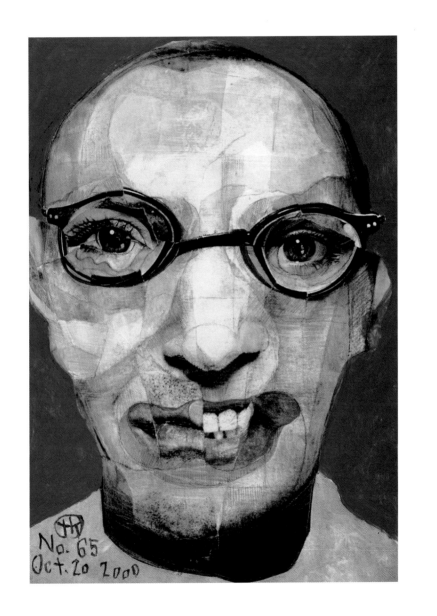

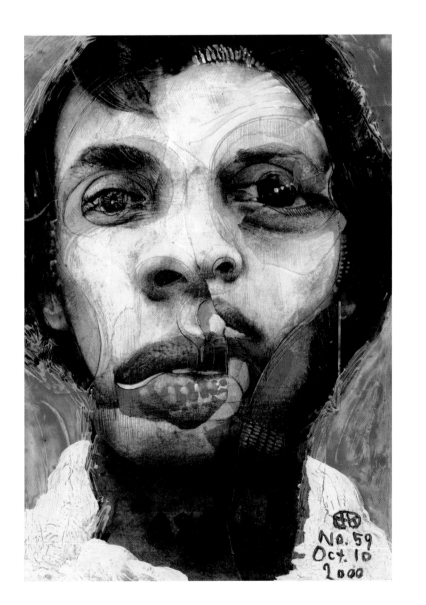

No. 59
Oct. 10
2000

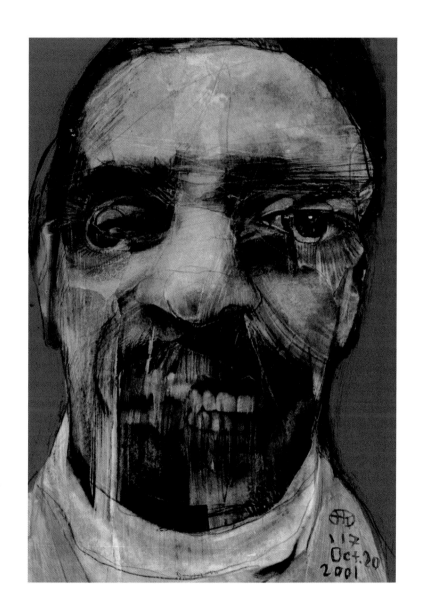

No. 53
Aug. 12
2000

No.95
MAR.6
2001

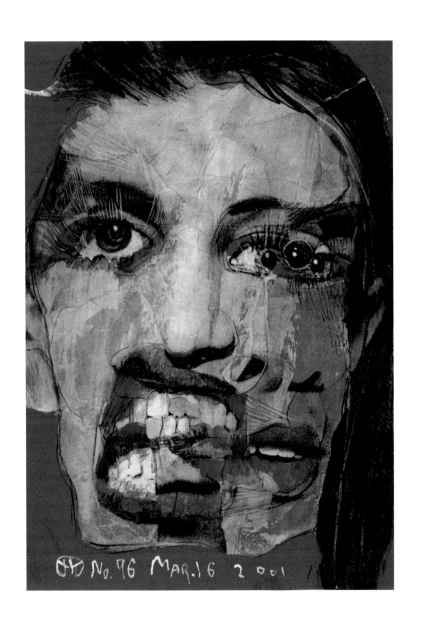

No 96
2000 July 16